THE GOOD BEHAVIOR BOOK FOR DOGS

THE GOOD BEHAVIOR BOOK FOR

DOGS

The Most Annoying Dog Behaviors . . . Solved!

GLOUCESTER MASSACHUSETTS

QUARRY BOOKS

Colleen Paige

Photography by J. Nichole Smith

First published in the United States of America by
Quarry Books, a member of
Quayside Publishing Group
33 Commercial Street
Gloucester, Massachusetts 01930-5089
Telephone: (978) 282-9590
Fax: (978) 283-2742
www.quarrybooks.com

Library of Congress Cataloging-in-Publication Data

Paige, Colleen.
    The good behavior book for dogs : the most annoying dog behaviors solved! / Colleen
  Paige ; photography by J. Nichole Smith.
        p.   cm.
    Includes index.
    ISBN-13: 978-1-59253-335-0
    ISBN-10: 1-59253-335-3
    1. Dogs--Behavior. 2. Dogs—Training. I. Title.
  SF433.P34 2007

                                    636.7'0887—dc22
                                    2006100320

ISBN-13: 978-1-59253-335-0
ISBN-10: 1-59253-335-3

10 9 8 7 6 5 4 3 2 1

The Good Behavior Book for Dogs contains a variety of training recommendations for your dog. While caution was taken to give safe recommendations, it is impossible to predict an individual dog's reaction to the recommended handling or training. Neither the author, Colleen Paige, nor the Publisher, Quayside Publishing Group, accepts liability for any mental, financial, or physical harm that arises from following the advice, techniques, or procedures in this book. Readers should use personal judgment when applying the recommendations of this text.

Design: Dutton & Sherman
Illustrations by Colleen Hanlon

Printed in Singapore

This book is dedicated to my amazing husband and son, my angels, who lovingly supported me and catered to all my needs as I lived in front of my computer for months to create it.

To my mother and father, who were there to help me rescue my first soul in need, and who taught me about compassion for all living things.

It is also dedicated to the memory of Spike, the dog who loved me unconditionally—despite my horrible shortcomings and ignorance—and who's cheering me on every time I rescue another soul. When one crosses the rainbow bridge, he's there to lead them home.

A special dedication to the memory of Steve Irwin, a man who gave great hugs, loved his family like no other, and changed the planet for animals. He will be greatly missed.

"I have no fear of losing my life—if I have to save a koala or a crocodile or a kangaroo or a snake, mate, I will save it."

—Steve Irwin

Contents

Foreword

Artist, writer, singer, and dog trainer Colleen Paige, has been delighting *Fido Friendly* magazine readers for years with her compassionate and humorous approach to coaching dogs in proper canine behavior. With her many years as a dog-lifestyle trainer, Colleen's unique style is something we can all mirror in our day-to-day lives when training our dogs.

In *The Good Behavior Book for Dogs*, Colleen uses typical examples that we, as dog guardians, face when training our furry companions, and she encourages us to have fun when working with our dogs and to put ourselves in the canine role as much as possible. By doing so, we can more easily see our dog's perspective. You'll learn, thanks to Colleen's guidance, that although it seems like at times our dogs may not be listening, they are listening—we are just not speaking their language.

Colleen starts us off on the right foot—or paw—by discussing proper nutrition for Fido and how to determine the right kind of exercise based on your dog's age and breed. As a guardian of two active labs, I can tell you from personal experience that exercise and diet have made all the difference in the behavior and health of my two fur children. As "Directors of Barketing" for *Fido Friendly* magazine, Zoey and Mattie have to have their best paws forward at all times. They are always staying at Fido-friendly hotels and mingling with people and their dogs. Colleen's advice has been invaluable in helping us train Zoey and Mattie to maintain a sense of decorum and to pay attention to what I am telling them. They may not understand what I am saying, but they know what I mean.

Each subsequent chapter deals with a specific behavioral problem, and offers tips and case studies along with Colleen's remedy. By reading *The Good Behavior Book for Dogs* and following Colleen's common sense and humorous approach to training dogs, you will have no other option than to be successful in helping your dog put his or her best paw forward. The reward for your consistent and hard work will be a faithful and loving companion who you will be able to enjoy for his or her lifetime.

—Susan Sims, Publisher, *Fido Friendly* magazine

Co-founder and publisher of seven-year-old Fido Friendly *magazine, the travel magazine for you and your dog. Susan and her husband, along with their two "Directors of Barketing," Zoey and Mattie, travel across the United States to sniff out hotels for purpose of review.*

Introduction

I DIDN'T PLAN TO BECOME A DOG TRAINER. I was a singer, fully engaged in a successful career and recording an album. But my life changed one day when I went through a windshield and almost died. To help me recover, I adopted a dog named Spike, whose life—and tragic death—made me vow to change the lives of dogs everywhere. It became my obsession.

I was a young woman, living alone and recovering slowly, when I decided I needed a healing and protective companion. I was hoping for someone like Clark Gable (well a girl can dream, can't she?), but when the opportunity arose to share my digs with a homeless two-year-old German shepherd named Spike—even though he had extreme halitosis, pointy ears, and a hairy belly—I felt it was kismet.

I wasn't really in a position to have a canine roommate in my small apartment, but my heart sheared in half at the thought of him being euthanized at the shelter. I imagined Spike sitting, watching the parade of people, hoping that some love-struck girl would catch the glimmer of magic in his eyes as she approached, but who would be led away by a parent who spotted a more appropriate dog. Many dogs escape this sad place, not into the arms of a new loving family but to a cold, damp room, for their final breath and a trip to the rainbow bridge.

I agreed to keep Spike and was really excited about the decision, but I questioned my mental health for thinking I could keep a 120-lb. German shepherd in an 800-square-foot (244 sq m) condo. Spike was a wonderful companion and an excellent protector, proving himself on more than one occasion: once, when he dislodged a gun from the belt of my roommate's boyfriend, and again, when he "discouraged" an intruder from kicking down my door at 3:00 AM. I loved this dog.

Defining Our Roles

I had had Spike for a year, and was recovering slowly, when I had a setback and wasn't able to walk him for long periods of time. As time went on, Spike's lack of socialization and exercise caused him to start chewing on and destroying my personal items, such as shoes, handbags, and furniture. He would also leave huge piles of poop throughout the house. (The fact that I left him a *bucket* of dog chow to nibble on all day might have had something to do with it.) In my ignorance, I assumed that this was what happened to everyone without a backyard, and I would just have to get used to it. But, every day, I came home and spent an hour cleaning up. I yelled at him, shoved his nose in it, then cried and apologized to him from the guilt of being so angry. I deodorized the carpet daily, until even the underground parking garage smelled like Lysol. It was a nightmare. I knew I had bitten off more than I could chew, but I couldn't give him back, and there was no way I was taking him to the shelter.

A Turn for the Worse

The final straw was arriving home to find that he had devoured my brand-new cowboy boots, leaving only the two heels sitting in the middle of the living room floor. Convinced that he had done this purposely because I had left him alone all day, I rolled up a newspaper and swatted him twice on the rear. I immediately felt horrible. This dog, who could rip my throat out in a split second, just sat there, shivering, whining, and looking pathetic. I was shamed of myself. I held him, crying and telling him how sorry I was.

Although potty and chewing incidents continued to happen, I never struck him again. I knew he wasn't getting what he needed, but I didn't know what to do. Then he attacked another tenant's dog in my parking garage. Although he caused minimal injury—I grabbed him off the other dog at the speed of light—I received a letter from the apartment manager, giving me 24 hours to find Spike a new home, or get out.

A friend's boyfriend said his parents would love to provide Spike with a new and loving home, complete with a yard and children to play with. Although it seemed a godsend, I felt like I was abandoning him. Letting him go was one of the most difficult decisions I have ever made. The next day, I accompanied Spike to my friend's car, the fur on his neck still damp from my tears. I kept crying as I watched him stare at me through the back window until he was out of sight.

A year went by. I couldn't bring myself to see him because I wanted him to acclimate to his new home. I was told he was happy and was doing nicely. It was the only solace I had. One night, I dreamed about him, awakening the next morning with a tug at my heart, as if it were a sign that he needed me. I decided to visit him.

I arrived at the house and was introduced to the family. After the usual greetings, I asked, "Where's my boy-boy?" The father gestured toward the back door, and I went out, then lost my breath. There I stood, hoping that Spike would remember me, when I was blasted by the smell of urine and excrement. Chained to a car in the middle of this junkyard was a filthy, emaciated dog—it was my Spike. He had no blanket, no doghouse, just a tub filled with black water and an old, dry bone.

A Day of Reckoning

Here was the love of my life—and I had done this to him. I should have met the family first. I should have taken him to the shelter and told them I would take him back if they couldn't find a home for him. In desperation, I offered the family money to buy him back, but was refused. I filed an abuse report with animal control, but got nowhere. Spike lived like that for several more years, until, I believe, he could no longer stand the misery. I made a promise to him to do everything I could to educate people and prevent another dog from having to live and die like he did.

My opportunity came a year later, when I met a dog trainer. His dog, ironically a German shepherd, spied me from the other end of a hallway, took off like a gazelle, and pinned me against the wall, licking my face. The dog trainer was apologetic but bewildered at his borderline aloof-and-protective dog's sudden endearment of me. He told me I had a gift with animals, and asked if I would like to learn how to train dogs. Only a few days later, I started my amazing journey at the National Institute of Dog Training under the brilliant teachings of Matthew "Uncle Matty" Margolis.

I trained in all levels of obedience and protection, and went on to work with law enforcement dogs, search-and-rescue dogs, and celebrity-protection dogs. I worked as a veterinarian technician in a busy Los Angeles animal trauma center, and after some intensive schoolwork, received my associate of applied science degree. I went on to work as a paramedic for six years, while continuing my dog training.

Answering My Calling

Eventually, the animals won me over completely. Thirteen more years of university study, coupled with ten years of research and hands-on caretaking of wolves, tigers, bears, dolphins, and elephants, brought me to where I am today.

This book is as much about helping you as it is about helping your dog. It's about having fun while you learn, giving you alternatives when possible, and helping you let go of the guilt and everyday stress that living with your dog causes you. No matter how good a parent you are, your little ones (children and dogs alike) are bound to act up at the most inopportune times and places. Part of being a good dog parent is not to sweat it if your pooch isn't perfect. Too many dog parents get unnecessarily strung out over their furry charges' behavior. Just let it go. Kids are kids, even if they are dogs. Think of me as a "*Dog*vorce Attorney," always trying to get her clients back together.

The reality of living with a dog is this: you will have dog hair on your mohair, you will need fragrant candles, and you will occasionally feel the need to ask, "What's that smell?" Most of all, though, you will have unconditional love. Join me on a journey into the "Whimsical World of Dog."

Chapter One

Maintaining Nutrition and Exercise

Proper nutrition and exercise are crucial to your dog's health. In fact, food is more essential to your dog's well-being than family, warmth, comfort, or toys. If you get this element of your dog's life right, the rest will fall into place much more easily. If you get it wrong, however, you may struggle with behavior issues that no training can help to control. When his diet goes astray, so can your dog. Start off on the right foot by making sure he eats well.

Second only to nutrition in importance is exercise. Providing the right kind of exercise for your dog's age and breed helps maintain a well-balanced body and releases pent-up energy. It can also ease stress and anxiety and can help your dog gain success in obedience training.

Nutrition

Provide food and treats made with whole grains and no chemical preservatives.

LET'S THINK, FOR A MOMENT, ABOUT BUILDING A house. To ensure your structure will withstand the stresses it will be subjected to, you must start with a strong foundation. A deficient nutritional foundation undermines your dog's behavior and physical health, and sabotages opportunities for him to learn and behave like a well-mannered pooch. Fortunately, fixing nutritional issues is easy, because when it comes down to it, dogs simply enjoy food—of any kind. They will beg for it, steal it, hide it, and even bury it.

Although a whole, organic, *handmade* doggy diet tops every canine's wish list, creating homemade dog dinners may not be realistic for today's busy families. Putting three hours a day into grinding chicken necks, filleting goose livers, and sautéing beef might be entertaining for some people, but many of us are just too busy to spend that much time in the kitchen for Fido. This leaves him facing the usual bowl of dry commercial kibble day in and day out, rather than the meaty dinner he had hoped for. It's not hard to understand why he doesn't leap for joy at every meal. (Would you?) Ever optimistic, poor Fido can only hope that another day will bring a more diverse menu. And so it should.

Not only can a boring menu give your dog the blues, but poor-quality dog food can be the sole cause of behavior problems. It's as imperative to nourish our dogs with high-quality, nutritionally dense foods as it is to provide *our* brains and bodies with a healthy diet. Consider the behavior of a child who eats processed sugar all day long. Most likely, this child will have poor health and severe attention-span issues, especially when it comes to learning. We can talk to children and help them make the right choices. Your dog depends on you to make the choices for him.

How can you save time in the kitchen and still make your dog happy? If you can afford it, buy high-quality, all-natural dry dog food, which can be found at pet stores or online, and mix it with ingredients such as good-quality wet dog food, mashed pumpkin, sweet potato, yogurt, green beans, carrots, peas, avocado, ground turkey, organic chicken stock, or boiled giblets. If you can't find all-natural dog food, buy the best-quality commercial brand available from your local supermarket. Each night, add something new to it. Keep a food diary noting how much your dog ate during that meal to help you remember which foods he seemed to like the most. You should also monitor bowel movements after each new food is introduced, to make sure the food is agreeable with your dog's tummy.

Food Allergies and Behavior

The most common causes of canine food allergies are ingredients I call the "No-No's." These ingredients, which include meat by-products, corn, wheat, salt, sugar, and chemical preservatives, are often responsible for allergic reactions, such as itchy skin, weepy eyes, ear infections, flatulence, irritated anal glands (running bottom over carpet), rashes, hot spots, and excessive bodily licking, especially around the feet and belly (*see* Ingredients to Avoid in Dog Food and Treats, page 19). Repeated exposure to large quantities of allergens in food can cause long-term chronic illnesses, infections, and behavior problems.

If you suspect your dog's food may be giving him allergies, you can try feeding a special diet to determine what is giving him trouble. The diet is composed of food that is scientifically created with very-low-molecular-weight proteins. (Proteins below a certain molecular weight are thought to be incapable of causing food allergies.) You can find this food, in wet and dry formulas, online and at many veterinarians' offices (*see* Resources, page 170). If, after six weeks of feeding this special diet, you find that your dog's allergy symptoms are alleviated, it's safe to assume that his food is the cause of his symptoms.

To determine which ingredient is the culprit (usually by-products from meat and poultry sources), reintroduce each one into the diet to see if your dog's symptoms recur. Check the ingredients list on your regular dog food label, and add each item—chicken, turkey, corn, bulgur wheat, potato, or rice, for example—into the special diet one at a time, every three weeks. At each meal, add ten percent of the test food to the bowl, and reduce the special diet by ten percent. Obviously, you won't be testing chemicals (BHT and BHA) or by-products (intestines, beaks, udders, esophagi, and often diseased and cancerous animal parts), but you can eliminate quite a few ingredients once you have determined which ones caused the allergy.

If your dog has no reaction to the added ingredients, the culprit is likely a chemical or by-product—which you will want to eliminate along with corn, wheat, sugar, and salt from your dog's diet, indefinitely. Don't be surprised, however, if you find that several ingredients cause a reaction. Once you've discovered the allergens, search out high-quality dog foods that do not contain these ingredients. Your dog may find an allergy-free or vet-recommended diet to be

Minimizing the amount of corn, wheat, salt, sugar, and chemical preservatives in your dog's diet will make him feel healthier and less hungry.

INGREDIENTS TO AVOID IN DOG FOOD AND TREATS

Your dog was meant to eat proteins, fats, and vegetables, not processed sugar, wheat, and corn. Many manufacturers also preserve their products by adding salt or sodium. This increases the dog's salt intake, and too much salt is just as bad for dogs as it is for humans.

Read the ingredient lists for dog foods and treats carefully. Even if salt is not listed as an ingredient, many treats are riddled with salt-laden foods, such as bacon.

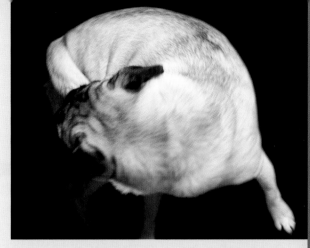

Dog food containing chemical preservatives, such as BHT, BHA, and ethoxyquin, can cause serious physical and behavioral problems.

Ingredient	Commonly Listed As
Butylated hydroxyanisole	BHA
Butylated hydroxytoluene	BHT
Ethoxyquin	Ethoxyquin
Artificial color	Including, but not limited to, red, blue, and yellow dyes
Artificial flavors	Including, but not limited to, beef, chicken, salmon, turkey, peanut butter, chocolate, and almond
Corn	Corn meal, corn gluten meal, corn germ meal, kibbled corn, ground yellow corn
Wheat	Wheat bran, bran, wheat germ, wheat gluten, wheat malt, wheat starch, whole wheat flour, gelatinized starch, modified food starch, hydrolyzed vegetable protein, starch, modified starch, vegetable gum, vegetable starch
Salt	Sea salt, sodium, bacon, anchovy, soy sauce
Sugar	Honey, sucrose, corn syrup, cane sugar, glucose, lactose, maltose
By-products	Including, but not limited to, lungs, spleen, kidneys, brain, livers, blood, bone, fatty tissue, stomachs, and intestines

bland, but a bland diet is better than a miserable dog! As long as he is drinking plenty of water, don't be alarmed if he doesn't take to it right away. When he gets hungry enough, he'll venture in for a nibble. Eventually, he'll adjust to his new diet, especially if you compensate with some yummy, allergy-free treats!

Sugar Blues

In addition to causing food allergies, many of the No-No's also create a "sugar high," which affects your dog's mood, energy, and hunger levels. A sugar high can cause a dog to be hyper and unfocused, and a dog must be focused in order to learn. Many dogs are believed to have a form of attention deficit hyperactivity disorder (ADHD); however, because little is known about this disorder in dogs, owners continue to think that their dogs are just ill-mannered and uncooperative, when, in fact, their behavior may be food-related.

In their normal daily cycle, dogs are energetic in the mornings and evenings, with the afternoon hours left for napping and lounging. This cycle is disturbed when a dog is fed food containing the No-No's. Corn and wheat quickly trans-form themselves into glucose in the bloodstream, and approximately 20 min-utes after eating, your dog will experience a sugar high. The high is followed, a couple of hours later, by a sugar low, which can make him sleepy, lethargic, moody, and irritable, and will often give him a feeling of malaise. Another symptom of a sugar low is hunger, often the cause of poor behavior in a dog that eats only twice a day, in the morning and the evening. Although this is a normal food schedule for most dogs, if yours is eating the wrong kind of food, he'll quickly become hungry again, making any pillow look to him like a piece of beef jerky.

Most problems that occur at home in the owner's absence can be cured by sim-ply eliminating the No-No's. I also suggest feeding your dog as close to your exit and as late at night as possible, especially if "hunger behavior" is destroying your house. Also try leaving safe bones and safe, long-lasting chew treats for your dog to enjoy during the day while you're gone.

Chemical Culprits

Many dog foods contain unnecessary chemical preservatives, such as butylated hydroxyanisole (BHA), butylated hydroxytoluene (BHT), and ethoxyquin. Although human food also contains BHA and BHT, we consume much less than a dog does in his average 15-year life span. It's one thing to have an occasional snack con-taining these preservatives; it's another thing to ingest them with every meal.

According to the Bureau of Chemical Safety in Ottawa, Canada, long-term feed-ing of BHT to rats and mice has been linked to an increase in the incidence of liver tumors. In fact, cancer is the number one killer of dogs today. Most people are horrified to learn this and not only start to pay more attention to their dog's diet but to their own, as well. Before chemically saturated dog food was introduced to the market, and dogs were eating veggies, meat, and potatoes, most lived to be 18 to 22 years of age. These days, depending on the breed, most dogs are considered old if they reach twelve or thirteen.

Ethoxyquin, first used as a rubber stabilizer in the 1950s, has also been used as a pesticide and an insecticide. It was originally used to preserve alfalfa clover and grasses for livestock feed. Since dog food falls under the same category as "feed," it has become a common preservative in dog food. The maximum allowable "safe" ethoxyquin residue in eggs, meat, and fruits for human consumption is 0.5 parts per million (ppm). In animal food, the maximum allowable concentration is 150 ppm. When you consider that dogs are much smaller than people, how safe is it for a dog weighing as little as eight pounds to ingest this every day?

Chemical preservatives are more commonly used by large manufacturers because their products are made in huge quantities and distributed all over the world, often sitting for long periods of time on store shelves or in warehouses where extreme temperatures can alter the quality of the product. Dog foods containing all-natural preservative alternatives, such as vitamin E or ascorbic acid (more commonly known as vitamin C) are available, but they don't hold up as long. That's why all-natural pet food manufacturers produce smaller quantities—so their product is more likely to stay fresh until sold.

Dog food preserved with mixed tocopherols (a form of vitamin E) generally has a shelf life of about six months, so use this kind of dog food right away. If you're looking for a new food for your pooch, visit a pet-food store and ask an employee to recommend a food devoid of the ingredients discussed in this chapter.

Changing the Diet

I recommend switching dog foods gradually. Switching food too abruptly can cause diarrhea and intestinal upset by creating an imbalance of bad and good intestinal bacteria, called "flora." Flora are naturally occurring bacteria that help to fight harmful bacteria and assimilate food, enzymes, and toxic elements consumed in food and water.

When harmful intestinal bacteria multiply, they produce large amounts of toxins and carcinogens. These toxins inhibit the normal function of the digestive system and increase the demands placed on the liver and kidneys, shortening your dog's life span, increasing his chances of getting cancer, and leading to various diseases and digestion problems. Dogs with high concentrations of beneficial bacteria are better equipped to fight the growth of unhealthy organisms and lead longer, healthier lives.

The flora in your dog's digestive system becomes familiar to the food and enzymes traveling through their neighborhood every day. But they are sensitive to pH changes, and with certain dogs, even the slightest change in diet can kill

THE WORLD'S OLDEST DOG

As of August 2006 the world's oldest dog was Jerry, an Australian red heeler–bull terrier cross that was fed kangaroo and emu meat. He was reported back in August of 2004 to be 27 years old. The oldest dog on record was an Australian cattle dog named Bluey, who died in 1939 at the age of 29. Now, I would not encourage you to feed your dog kangaroo and emu meat, but it just goes to show how dogs that eat a healthy diet can live longer than they would on chemical-filled commercial food.

Above: Always introduce new food slowly, over a period of seven to ten days, to avoid stomach upset and diarrhea.

Right: Don't "baby" picky eaters—you will only make the problem worse.

the good flora, allowing bad bacteria to thrive and cause illness. Why would you want to switch foods? Changing your dog's diet slowly gives the flora a chance to adjust, reducing the chance of stomach and intestinal distress. To change your dog's diet slowly, add different, tested ingredients to your dog's usual dry kibble over a period of seven to ten days. Add a higher percentage of new food to old, every day, until it is switched 100 percent.

I also suggest adding a *probiotic* supplement to your dog's diet, or buying food with probiotics in it. Probiotics are beneficial bacteria necessary for a healthy and balanced intestinal tract. So how do you know if your dog food contains probiotics? Look for ingredient names such as dried *Streptococcus faecium* fermentation product or dried *Lactobacillus acidophilus* fermentation product.

Picky Eaters

Just like kids, some dogs are picky eaters. If yours turns up his nose at meals you have slaved over in an attempt to appeal to his palate, it's possible that some of the foods you give him upset his tummy. Some dogs can be very

CALL YOUR VET IF:

- Your dog is not eat-
  ing or drinking water
  and has a warm, dry
  nose.
- Your dog, which usu-
  ally has a great
  appetite, has
  stopped eating for
  24 hours and refuses
  favorite treats
- Your dog eats, but
  can't keep food or
  water down and is
  frequently vomiting
  or has diarrhea
- Your dog has gone
  for more than 48
  hours without food,
  even if he is still
  drinking just fine.

To check for dehydra-
tion, pull up on the
scruff of your dog's
neck. In healthy,
hydrated dogs, the skin
fold springs back down
into place right away.
In dehydrated dogs, it
stays up in a ridge and
slowly flattens out.
Another symptom is a
very dry mouth.

sensitive to too much fat, giving them diarrhea, while others are nauseated by food allergies. Perhaps your dog simply dislikes his current brand of store-bought dog food. If your dog is picky, try switching to a better-quality, all-natural high-protein food. Why high-protein food? Because it contains more meat than fillers and when eaten, even in small amounts, will keep your dog satisfied longer than poor-quality sugar- and corn-laden kibble.

You might find that he doesn't take to his new food right away, and will refuse to eat it. Don't worry. Your dog will not starve if there is food in his bowl—especially if there is good food in it! He's just used to your doting and failed attempts to figure out what he likes. When he realizes that you aren't going to be the gallant gourmet any longer, he'll eat. I know this will be very difficult for many of you to handle, as he stares up with those sad eyes like you're being cruel, but don't give in, as it *will* pay off, and quickly!

Don't be tempted to offer food from your plate, either, or you may set up bad behavior. It may take a whole day for his kibble to disappear, but as long as he's still drinking water, don't be concerned.

Treats

It's easy to sabotage all the hard work you have done adjusting your dog's daily diet if you continue to feed unhealthy treats. Many people succeed in eliminating the No-No's from their dog's diet, then fail to change the treats as well, setting themselves up for poor results. Keep treats containing wheat, corn, and sugar to a minimum. If you give treats often, choose low-carb, high-protein nibbles to keep the weight off and avoid a sugar high. Try also to steer clear of treats containing salt or sodium—bacon, for example—and rawhide of any kind. This popular treat swells to five times its original size in your dog's stomach and takes up to two weeks to digest. This is a recipe for disaster, especially if you have an aggressive chewer, as it can cause an intestinal blockage resulting in serious illness and possibly death. Supplement with much safer and easily digestible treats, such as pigs' ears, pork hide chews, and compressed pork hide bones.

Treats are a great way to make your dog's training fun and help to keep him motivated to listen and comply.

TREATS CAN BE USED FOR

- Rewards
- Keeping your dog distracted from separation anxiety triggers before you leave
- Training your dog to go potty on command (see chapter three)
- Helping him to stay calm and focused in difficult situations
- Encouraging him to endure an uncomfortable situation
- Helping him to become desensitized to scary people or places

FUN WITH FRUITS, NUTS, AND VEGGIES

Supplement your dog's treat diet with the following fruits and veggies:

- Sweet potato
- Apples, whole and cored or sliced (be sure to remove all the seeds)
- Melon
- Avocado (avoid the pit; it can be toxic)
- Carrots
- Blueberries
- Peanut butter
- Spinach
- Tomatoes
- Bananas

BYE-BYE FLEAS! DOG BISCUITS

There are many dangers associated with chemical flea products. For more-natural "flea warfare," try these yummy snacks.

Ingredients:

- 2 cups (220–250 g) rye flour
- ½ cup (40 g) wheat germ
- ½ cup (40 g) brewer's yeast
- 2 cloves garlic, minced
- 3 tablespoons (45 ml) olive oil
- 1 cup (235 ml) unsalted organic chicken stock

Preheat oven to 325°F (163°C). Grease three nonstick baking sheets with olive oil or olive oil–flavored cooking spray. Combine the first three ingredients. In a large mixing bowl, combine garlic and oil. Slowly add flour mixture and stock alternately into oil and garlic mixture, beating well after each addition, until the dough is well mixed. Shape dough into a ball. On a lightly floured surface, roll out dough 12 inches (30.5 cm) wide. Using a 2-inch (5.1 cm) bone-shaped cookie cutter, cut dough. Lay biscuits on prepared baking sheets. Bake 20 to 25 minutes or until golden. Allow biscuits to cool for 20 minutes, then store in refrigerator or freezer.

You don't need to be a great chef to make dog treats that will get your pooch's tail wagging!

LIVER SNAPS

Dogs love liver, and these easy-to-make treats are full of protein to nourish the dog on the go! Limit servings to one (5 cookies) a week. Too much cooked liver can lead to vitamin A toxicity.

Ingredients:

- 1 pound (455 g) any kind of raw liver (preferably free-range, hormone- and antibiotic-free)
- 1 cup (80 g) Irish oatmeal
- 1 teaspoon (3 g) fresh minced garlic
- 2 free-range eggs
- ¼ cup (60 ml) plain organic yogurt
- ¼ cup (31 g) chopped walnuts

Preheat oven to 350°F (177°C). Puree liver and Irish oatmeal, and combine with remaining ingredients in a large bowl. Roll into cookie-sized portions, place on a nonstick cookie sheet, and flatten. Bake for 20 minutes. Allow to cool for 15 minutes and freeze. Feed frozen or at room temperature. Refrigerate leftovers.

AUNTIE COLLEEN'S SEASIDE BROWNIES

Do you have a fish-loving Fido? Cold-water fish such as salmon contain omega-3 fatty acids, which help to decrease "bad cholesterols" (LDLs and triglycerides) in the bloodstream. Omega-3 fatty acids also help to decrease the constriction of larger arteries, improving circulation and decreasing inflammation in blood vessels.

Ingredients:

- 1 pound (455 g) fresh or frozen wild salmon
- 1 tablespoon (5 g) garlic powder or minced garlic
- 2 free-range eggs
- 1½ cups (195 g) unbleached wheat or rye flour
- ¼ cup (20 g) organic grated parmesan cheese

Preheat oven to 350°F (177°C). Puree salmon, garlic, and eggs in food processor or blender (or mix in a bowl). Add wheat or rye flour and mix to a brownie-like consistency. Spread in a 9 x 9–inch (22.9 x 22.9 cm) greased pan. Bake for 20 minutes. When the brownies are done, they will have a soft, sticky texture, and the edges will pull away from the sides of the pan. Cut into squares and freeze. Feed warm or at room temperature. Refrigerate leftovers.

The following foods can be toxic to dogs. All the fruit pits listed contain cyanide.

- pear seeds (pips)
- plum kernels
- peaches and apricots
- apple seeds (pips)
- green potatoes and potato peels
- rhubarb leaves
- moldy foods
- alcohol
- yeast dough
- coffee grounds or beans, and tea
- hops (for brewing)
- tomato leaves and stems
- broccoli (in large amounts)
- raisins and grapes
- almonds
- chocolate
- cigarettes, tobacco, cigars

Offering treats can make a shy dog friendlier and more social.

Uses for Treats

Treats are a valuable tool when it comes to many aspects of your dog's relationship with you and the world around him. Treats work wonders for helping shy dogs overcome a fear of strangers (as long as the dog is not prone to biting), can help get your dog to come to you when called, and keep the focus on you during training. I don't use treats as a "reward" for good behavior or compliance with a command; rather, I use them as a motivator to keep the dog encouraged and excited during training, with love and praise being the true reward at the end. Stagger how often you use treats for training and commands. This way, you prevent the cycle of your dog only complying when treats are in sight. When he does comply, always show praise with a pat on the head, a smile, and a "Good dog."

Along with food allergies, dogs can have environmental allergies, such as hay fever and rashes on the feet and tummy, from molds, grass seed, and pollen.

ENVIRONMENTAL ALLERGIES

Your dog's environment can also cause allergies. If your dog has weepy eyes or begins sneezing, scratching, and rolling his body around on the ground or carpet after walks through tall grass or flowers, he may suffer from environmental allergies. These allergies are triggered by many kinds of mold, pollen, and grass seed all year round but generally cause fewer symptoms in winter.

Eliminating chemical preservatives in the diet can help relieve environmental allergies, as well. Because a body overloaded with chemicals is always in "inflammatory mode," it has a difficult time when exposed to histamines, the proteins that cause inflammation. To help keep your dog's coat allergy-free, clean dirt and residue from his body daily, using wipes made especially for dogs, and avoid washing your dog more than twice a week. Daily or frequent washing (three to five times a week) dries out your dog's skin and further aggravates skin allergy symptoms. Instead, bathe your dog twice a week, and add a skin soother, such as tea tree oil or colloidal oatmeal, to the water. If you suspect that your dog has dry skin, add a teaspoon (half a teaspoon for little dogs) of olive or flaxseed oil to his dog food every day. Consult your veterinarian for ways to reduce allergens in your dog's environment and for natural remedies or medications to control symptoms.

Exercise

Dog agility, a fun and competitive sport, is a great way to help your dog overcome boredom and self-esteem issues.

EXERCISE IS AS IMPORTANT to dogs as it is to us—maybe even more so. Walking a dog is rarely enough, as most dogs could walk all day long and still not get the kind of outlet they crave. Dogs that suffer from a lack of daily aerobic exercise are often the same dogs that exhibit behavioral problems. A lack of exercise may be to blame for fifty percent of your dog's behavioral problems. When your dog has had the proper release of energy, problems such as jumping, digging, barking, anxiety, destructive behavior, and aggression often abate.

Pay close attention to how much daily exercise your dog needs, taking into consideration the age of your dog, the breed, the season, and the exercise itself. It is crucial to not overdo it. Small dogs with short legs usually don't need to be run on a daily basis, while racing breeds such as greyhounds and whippets may need to be run several times a day. Short-nosed breeds, such as bulldogs, boxers, and pugs, have more difficulty breathing when they run too hard.

SIGNS OF A HAPPY DOG:

- Barking or whining, combined with running back and forth and jumping
- Body: relaxed, lying with one paw tucked under body or lying playfully on back
- Body: in a bow, front end down, rear end up
- Mouth: panting with happy expression, as if smiling
- Tail: thumping on floor, wagging enthusiastically

Healthy Games to Play

The following is a list of games requiring few accessories that you can easily play with your dog.

Hide and Seek

Command your dog to stay, while you continue to repeat the command and sneak off into another room. Once positioned, call out "Come 'n' get me!" When your dog locates you, jump out, being careful not to scare him, and praise him for finding you. Repeat as long as he seems to be having fun. Offering a treat or a favorite toy when he successfully finds you is another fun addition to the game!

Tug O' War

Pretty self-explanatory; if playing with a puppy, be careful of loose teeth—pulling them out prematurely may hurt his gums. If you have a dominant dog, make sure you always win!

Fetch

A great game to play, whether at a lake or beach, or simply on the grass in a park or backyard, fetch is a good aerobic exercise that can also be played indoors during hot or inclement weather. While most dogs have no problem chasing and picking up a ball, some will run away with, rather than return, the object. To discourage this, attach your dog to a long line run in the yard, then toss the ball or other toy, making sure you don't throw it out of range. A fun fetch game for "flighty" dogs is to put them on the line run and attach a rag or stuffed animal to an old fishing pole, whipping it back and forth for major chase enjoyment.

Treasure Hunt

Hide a toy or a treat in tall grass or under a pillow, can, box, blanket, or other safe object that Fido can flip over to uncover his prize!

Playing treasure hunt outdoors can be a great way for you and your dog to get some much-needed exercise!

How Exercise Affects Training

Exercising your dog before training sessions can be a dog owner's best tool for getting Fido to comply. Before training sessions, walk or run your dog long enough that you are confident some steam has been blown off. As with regular exercise, however, don't overdo it. An adolescent dog might have the energy for several walks and training sessions a day but lacks the concentration level for it, whereas an older dog can concentrate just fine but should not be subjected to rigorous workouts.

Avoid feeding your dog within an hour of training, and be sure to use protein-rich, low-sugar treats during your sessions. Do not feed too many treats during

When your dog seems hyper, even a short game of fetch will allow him to let off steam and help him behave better.

training; cookies and jerky broken into pea-sized bits should be sufficient. A good rule of thumb is to feed no more than three wafer-sized treats and two, 3-inch (7.6 cm) jerky sticks per day during training.

If throwing a ball or Frisbee doesn't appeal to your pal, try a different route, such as going to a dog park where he can romp with others of his kind; taking him swimming; or partaking in agility classes. I often recommend doggy day care or dog-walking services if you find that you have little or no time to exercise your dog.

Keep training sessions to no more than 10 minutes at a time and no more than 25 minutes in total. Keep the physical play going with your dog between sessions, to make sure that energy levels and boredom don't sabotage your valuable time together. If treats don't appear to be a motivator during training, try using a ball or a favorite toy to keep your dog focused on you and motivated for the next round. Before you begin any new physical play or exercise routine, make sure your dog has had a recent checkup to ensure that his heart, lungs, and joints are healthy.

Exercise is an important part of your dog's well-being. A tired dog is a happy dog.

Fitness, Health, and Travel

YOUR DOG MAY BE YOUR CONSTANT COMPANION—even when you travel. Today, many commercial airlines, resorts, hotels, and restaurants are specifically catering to Fido during travel and vacation getaways, making it easier than ever to have a *paws*itively great trip!

Before you travel with Fido, whether by car, boat, or plane, make sure he is fully exercised.

Air Travel

Be sure your dog has a physical exam prior to flying—a health certificate is required by many commercial airlines. A check-up is essential if your pooch hasn't had one in the last year; an up-to-date exam not only provides a baseline health reference for future checkups, it can uncover a problem you might not have been aware of. Altitude changes can cause an underlying asymptomatic problem to suddenly become symptomatic while your dog is in the crate, and medical issues, such as high blood pressure, ear infections, and cardiac problems, can become aggravated.

Dog owners often resort to giving their dogs tranquilizers to alleviate stress when they fly, but tranquilization is considered controversial, as high altitudes can exacerbate the effect and create problems. Bach Flower Remedy, a homeopathic alternative, has been proven to help sensitive animals, such as dogs, cats, and birds, overcome stress and anxiety. Bach Flower Remedy is a combination of rockrose, impatiens, clematis, star-of-Bethlehem, and cherry plum flower remedies. The ingredients work to relieve acute stress, anxiety, and panic attacks. Created by British homeopathic doctor Edward Bach in the 1930s, it is nontoxic, doesn't sedate your dog, and has no side effects. Administer the remedy daily, three weeks prior to travel, directly into your dog's mouth. Be consistent about dosage and schedule, making sure not to miss a day. You may not notice a difference immediately, as it can take up to two weeks to take full effect. Always check with your veterinarian before offering any remedies or medication. Bach Flower Remedy is available online and at most nutritional stores (*see* Resources, page 170).

Another helpful approach for calming a nervous dog is the use of canine massage, one or two days prior to the trip. Canine massage increases circulation, relieves muscle tension and anxiety, relaxes muscle spasms, and increases range of motion. The calming benefits can last for days. An older animal that has been confined for long periods of time during travel can really benefit from massage afterwards, to relieve stiff joints and muscles. It is a great treat to incorporate into your pet's life!

Be sure to include your dog's favorite toy or blanket for an easier trip.

Put a blanket and an old T-shirt with your scent on it in the travel crate, so your dog can feel comfortable and more secure in your absence. However, if your dog is prone to chewing items, do not include comfort items, such as blankets, stuffed toys, or clothing, to avoid the risk of choking.

Feeding and Exercise

Food, as well as any medications, should be given at least a couple of hours prior to any flight, to avoid upset tummy or nervous vomiting. A treat toy filled with all-natural peanut butter will keep your dog busy licking for a few thousand miles and help combat boredom. Baby food is a great alternative to peanut butter in a treat toy. Limit water if your flight is longer than a few hours, because peanut butter can cause your dog to drink too much of it.

Exercise your dog prior to any trip in which he will be confined for long periods of time. To make sure that your dog does not emerge from his crate with painfully stiff joints, don't exercise him too much or too soon before travel; allow several hours to pass, to give his joints a chance to relax and cool down before confinement.

JASMINE'S STORY

Grief can cause a dog to lose his interest in both food and exercise, as Angie discovered after her divorce. Jasmine, her three-year-old golden retriever, missed her Daddy, John, and her canine sibling, Hunter, who went with John when he left. Angie got Jasmine and the car; John got Hunter and the exercise equipment. Although Jasmine escaped the turmoil of having to relocate from the only home she ever knew, she seemed depressed and confused. She missed her daily jogs with Hunter and John, and the romps with Hunter in the garden, chasing squirrels and each other. Her world now was silent and still.

Noticing her pooch's melancholy, Angie brought home Jasmine's favorite treats from the local *bark*-ery, even cooking her special gourmet meals, only to watch Jasmine apathetically turn her nose up at everything. It had been two weeks since John left, and Jasmine had eaten on—maybe—four occasions. Not only was she looking pitifully sad, but she was getting thin from not eating, a symptom of grief in social animals.

When it came to walks, Jasmine, who used to leave home with enthusiasm and eagerness to explore the neighborhood, now walked half a block, eliminated, and then turned around, as if to indicate that she was tired and had had enough walking. In fact, she was tired—she was becoming malnourished. Angie called the vet, who suggested that Jasmine's sprit, along with her appetite, would recover with time and Angie was not to worry. In the meantime, she should make sure that Jasmine was drinking water, which she was.

Several weeks went by, and Jasmine had lost about seven pounds. Desperate, Angie called me for help. I suggested that Jasmine needed some fun and, even more importantly, a distraction. I suggested doggy day care. I felt that, because she used to be such a playful dog and was only three years old, she still had plenty of spunk left in her—she just needed to be gently reminded of it.

The first few days at day care were a bit unnerving for Jasmine. She really didn't want to have anything to do with any of the other dogs, and, for the first time in her life, she actually nipped at several that approached with an invitation to romp. The employees were able to coax a few wags and kisses from her, but she mostly just sat with her chin on her paw and watched the other dogs.

Then she met Sam. New to the day care facility, Sam was also a golden retriever, and he looked very similar to Hunter. He was a playful boy, with a laughing smile, and he lit Jasmine up like a flare! She ran over to him and greeted him with a tail wag that could knock down an oak tree. She whined and whimpered and ran in circles. It was as if her brother had reappeared right in front of her! The spell was broken.

Not only did she return to her old self, she couldn't wait to get to day care every morning to play with Sam. Because of the increased daily activity, she was tired when she got home, but "happy tired." Not only did the experience of finding a new friend help her over her grief, the boost in endorphins (the happy brain chemicals) from the exercise helped her to stay happy and sleep well. She soon forgot about her grief and was back to being her happy self.

OBJECTS IN THE MIRROR ARE
LARGER THAN THEY APPEAR

Make frequent stops to avoid stiff joints in older dogs. Puppies need special attention and safety precautions while traveling.

Riding in Cars with Dogs

Having your pal accompany you on the road, whether for short or long trips, can be a whole lot of fun. Most dogs love the car and eagerly anticipate their next travel adventure with you. Before you hit the road, however, there are some things to keep in mind.

Keep your dog confined while in the car. You will find it difficult to concentrate on driving if your dog is overly excited, jumping back and forth, or suddenly becomes carsick. Safety is also a concern. Even when traveling at just 10 miles an hour, braking quickly to avoid an animal or person in the road subjects your dog to the risk of broken bones from being projected into the backseat, hitting the dashboard, or worse, getting ejected from the vehicle altogether. And no matter how competent you are as a driver or how routine it is to have your pal beside you at the wheel, neither of you is safe from irresponsible drivers. As a former paramedic in the busy city of Los Angeles, I responded to many accidents caused by drivers who were distracted by pets in the vehicle.

Using a safety harness or crate prevents injury to your dog. If you can't afford a safety harness, you can make a harness with rope and clips, or loop your dog's leash through the seatbelt to keep him from moving around.

Before you get Fido into the car, put down a towel where he will be seated. If he is prone to car sickness and vomits during the trip, you won't be dangerously distracted and can just ignore it until you get home. If you can possibly avoid it, don't put your dog into a car full of screaming children. This can make him very anxious and behave in a way that he normally wouldn't.

During the trip, pull into a rest stop every fifty miles or so to give your dog a chance to stretch, drink water, and go potty. This will prevent him from becoming too stressed and restless, which will lead him to dislike car travel. Frequent stops also help avoid car sickness. If your dog does have issues with car sickness, talk to your vet about giving him a motion sickness medication.

Offer your dog the same attention and safety you would give a child riding with you.

Chapter Two

Establishing Mutual Respect

Many people believe they understand everything their dogs do and why. (I can understand this—I thought I knew my child until he turned thirteen and proved me wrong.) You've taught your dog certain tricks and commands and believe you know the difference between his "hunger whine" and the "please let me in" whimper. This may, in some part, be true, but unless you have seriously studied dog behavior, it's likely that you don't know your dog as well as you think you do!

So, how can you fully understand your dog, an animal with no ability to speak the human language? The first thing you need to know is what an "Alpha" is.

Making eye contact with your dog is very important in establishing that you're the leader.

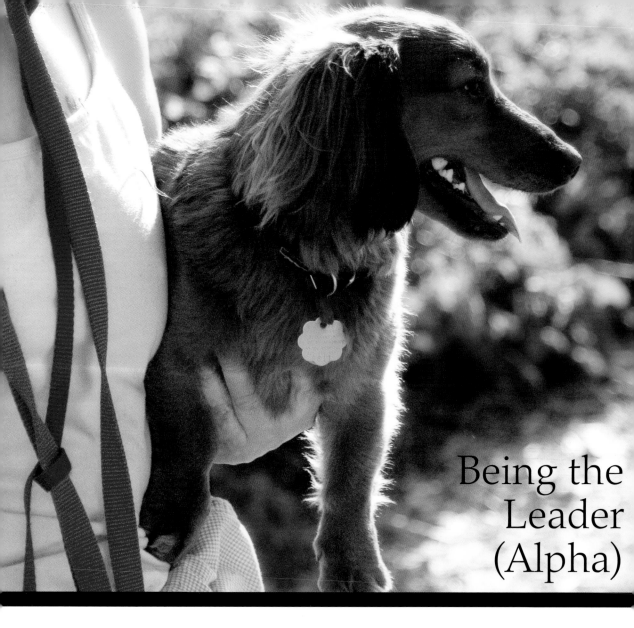

Being the Leader (Alpha)

THE WORD "ALPHA" (THE FIRST LETTER OF THE Greek alphabet) is defined as "something that is first." In the animal world, it describes the highest-ranked or most dominant individual of one's peer group. It does not necessarily refer just to dogs, although it has been used more than anything else in the subject of canine behavior—especially wolves. Your dog, although not a wolf, has social similarities to one: he needs a leader and views his human family and other dogs in the family as a pack.

Domestic dogs have some traits in common with wild dogs, and some show them more than others—especially if they are predatory and like to hunt, or are aggressive, dominant, and territorial. But they have great differences, as well. People often have the opinion—gained from articles, books, or uneducated dog trainers—that to get their dogs to behave, they need to treat them the way a wolf would treat a pack member: aggressively. I have studied, researched, been kissed by, and cared for wolves, and I can tell you that their social structure is quite different from that of domestic dogs. Wolves need to use aggression to survive; that is their nature, their programming. Dogs do not need aggression to survive, nor do they need people to use aggression to get them to comply.

Trouble occurs when your dog thinks he is the Alpha, because every pack must have one, and if you are not stepping up to the plate, your dog will do what comes naturally. If you behave as the Alpha, then you will be viewed as such by your dog, and he will comply with your commands. Will he test you from time to time? Absolutely— that is his nature. Humans and animals alike frequently test their environments and relationships in some way.

If your dog feels any doubt about whether or not you are strong enough to hold the Alpha position, he will continuously try to challenge you and other family members. Dogs are smart, and even dogs that are considered "dumb" catch on pretty quickly when Mom or Dad doesn't show consistency or discipline. In canine pack behavior, a younger dog will challenge the Alpha dog when he becomes old and weak. Eventually, the challenger wins, because the older Alpha isn't physically strong enough to hold the position anymore. This doesn't happen with human pack leaders, simply because a dog's life span is relatively short in comparison to our own, and we have the capability to always be the Alpha throughout the life of the dog.

Being dominant over your dog will not make him fear or dislike you, but there is a difference between being dominant and abusive. Dominant is establishing yourself as the leader by making him sit before food or play, not repeating commands, and using eye contact. Being abusive is yelling at or hitting him, rolling him over on his back, or getting in his face and bullying him, as some dog trainers teach you to do. Forcing your dog to roll on his back and submit, "because this is what an Alpha wolf would do," damages trust, can

injure the dog, creates a fear-based relationship, and removes any reason for your dog to comply out of respect and love for you. It's also a good way to get bitten in the face! Don't ever roll your dog over on his back to discipline him. It is simply the wrong approach.

Dogs feel secure when they know what to expect in their daily lives. Through teaching boundaries, our dogs feel safe and secure and know that they are loved. To teach boundaries to your dog, you must be clear and consistent and not let him get away with things. A dog needs to know that if he goes too far you *will* stop him. Not dealing with the problems on a consistent basis is what gets people into trouble.

It's fascinating to watch wolves. They are so mysterious and spiritual. Many people are tempted to own wolves or wolf hybrids because they want an intimidating, protective type of dog that is also a conversation piece. Unfortunately, most of time, the only conversation is about who he bit last.

People who own wolf hybrids end up having so much trouble with them that they usually need to euthanize the dogs to reduce the risk to friends, family members, and even themselves. Unless a person is trained and educated about wolves and domestic dogs, the person has no idea that he or she has a time-bomb on a leash. Issues usually result from not knowing how to deal with the dog in a balanced way, by being either too aggressive or not aggressive enough, until it ends in disaster.

Playful Respect

To keep your Alpha status, show your dog that he must work for the things he receives from you. Always make your dog sit before going out the door for a walk. This establishes that *you* are taking him for a walk and not vice versa. Use a leash if he's not off-leash trained. Make your dog sit before throwing a ball or stick. Again, this reinforces that he gets no play without first showing you respect.

Make him sit before you give him food or treats. Because food is a good motivator for dogs, this really establishes you as his leader and expresses to him that he has to depend on you for his survival and must work for the good things he gets. When he complies, give him loads of love and praise, which makes him want to work even harder for it.

If you have a dominant, aggressive, or overly zealous dog, never allow him to win at tug of war. Your losing only indicates to him that's he's stronger than you, and it will weaken your role as the Alpha. So if you play this game, make sure you have the muscle to back it up! On the other hand, if your dog is shy, has low self-esteem, or has been bullied by another dog, this is a great game to let him win. It will make him feel more confident, especially if you give him lots of love and praise him when he's won. But be sure you know that your dog could benefit from this game if you choose to let him win.

Treats are an instant motivator. Make him sit before giving, and show him love and praise.

Basic Training

TEACHING YOUR POOCH BASIC OBEDIENCE SKILLS can often be a challenge, especially if you've got a pesky puppy or a dog that wants to be king of the castle. If you're having behavior issues with your dog, don't put off obedience training—it may soon be too late to change bad habits that you and your dog have developed.

If you haven't already done so, research your dog's breed and become familiar with its basic characteristics, personality traits, and exercise requirements. Breed traits can help you understand why he behaves the way he does. If you have a mixed-breed dog, research as many breeds as you can identify your dog by and study them all. It shouldn't take long to figure out why your Jack Russell terrier/beagle mix is predatory, as both breeds were bred to hunt. If you have trouble identifying your dog's breed, ask your veterinarian for his or her opinion. If you have what appears to be a mixed breed, it shouldn't be difficult to single out at least one.

Tips for Successful Obedience Training

The most important part of obedience training is to get your dog to pay attention to you when asked. Start at home by calling his name periodically throughout the day. When he appears, give him a little treat or throw a toy and praise him for coming when called. Then go about your business. Make it casual and fun, and your dog will want to hear his name called all the time! Once he's consistent about giving you his attention when his name is called, you have mastered the first step in obedience training.

The next step is to *keep* his attention. When your dog is required to focus for more than a few minutes during training sessions, you may discover that he seems bored and easily distracted. The younger the dog, the more easily distracted he'll be, as he is still discovering the world around him. Avoid training your dog in a park or public place until he has learned to focus on you. Generally, your backyard or even your living room will be a perfect and quiet place for him to learn. Use motivators such as treats and toys to keep it fun and to keep his eyes on you.

Use eye contact to get your dog to pay attention and listen.

Patience, love, respect, and consistency are the keys to success.

MORE TIPS:

- Exercise patience. It is not your dog's desire to frustrate you or make you mad. Remember that he is learning, and with that comes the need for repetition. When you find yourself losing your temper over attention or ability issues, remind yourself how difficult it would be for *you* to learn a different language in a couple of days, taught by a teacher who hardly spoke your own language! Take a break, breathe deeply, and start again.

- Be creative. If your dog gets easily bored, mix up the motivators, like giving a treat for practicing one technique and using a ball for practicing another.

- Be happy. A happy tone of voice will communicate that you are not upset with him and that training is supposed to be fun. If he feels that you're happy with him, he'll work harder to keep that smile on your face.

- Be consistent. The most important tool for success is consistency. If you do not practice every day, your dog will forget what is expected of him. Try to make your training sessions last at least 15 to 20 minutes. However, even if you only have the time for 10 minutes one day and 20 minutes another, as long as you train every day, you will see results.

DOG BREED CATEGORIES

GUARD DOGS
Boxer
Bulldog
Bullmastiff
Dalmatian
Doberman
Giant Schnauzer
Great Dane
Keeshond
Miniature Schnauzer
Newfoundland
Rottweiler
Saint Bernard

GUN DOGS
Chesapeake Bay Retriever
Cocker Spaniel
English Setter
German Shorthaired Pointer
Golden Retriever
Irish Setter
Irish Water Spaniel
Labrador Retriever
Pointer
Weimaraner

HAULING DOGS
Alaskan Malamute
Samoyed
Siberian Husky

HEELING DOGS
Cardigan Corgi
Pembroke Corgi

HERDING DOGS
Australian Cattle Dog
Bearded Collie
Border Collie
German shepherd/Alsatian
Great Pyrenees
Miniature Collie
Old English Sheepdog
Rough Collie
Shetland Sheepdog
Smooth Collie

HUNTING TERRIERS
Airedale Terrier
Bedlington Terrier
Bull Terrier
Cairn Terrier
Fox Terrier, Smooth Coat
Fox Terrier, Wire Coat
Irish Terrier
Jack Russell Terrier
Kerry Blue Terrier
Scottish Terrier
West Highland White Terrier

RUNNING DOGS
Afghan Hound
Whippet
Borzoi
Deerhound
Greyhound
Irish Wolfhound

SCENT DOGS
Basenji
Basset Hound
Beagle
Bloodhound
Elkhound
Long-haired Dachshund
Smooth-haired Dachshund
Rhodesian Ridgeback

FOR FUN! SOME BASIC COMMANDS IN DIFFERENT LANGUAGES

SPANISH
Sit—*Siéntese*
Down—*Abajo*
Stay—*Estancia*
Come—*Aquí*

ITALIAN
Sit—*Siedasi*
Down—*Giù*
Stay—*Soggiorno*
Come—*Qui*

FRENCH
Sit—*Reposez-vous*
Down—*Vers le bas*
Stay—*Séjour*
Come—*Ici*

GAELIC
Sit—*Suigh*
Down—*Leag uait*
Stay—*Fan mar a
    bhfuil tú*
Come—Seo

Basic Training Commands

I LIKE TO USE TREATS AS A MOTIVATOR DURING training. However, they are not the reward for compliance—love and praise are. Soft, healthy, jerky-type treats are best, as they break into bite-sized pieces. This prevents overindulgence and keeps the dog from becoming distracted by the need to stop and "crunch." If you prefer to train "treat-free," have your dog focus on a ball or a favorite toy and encourage him to comply with your command in anticipation of receiving it.

Sit

The first command to teach your dog is *sit*. Use the word "sit" consistently, so he can relate the action to the word. I suggest you put a collar and leash on him for this, even if training in the house.

Start by holding the leash (not shown), and standing in front of your dog, making sure you have eye contact with him. If he's distracted, click your tongue or talk to him to refocus his attention on you. Hold a treat between your index finger and thumb and raise it above his head, moving it in the direction of his rump, and issue the sit command. Many dogs will sit naturally, just so they can watch your hand without straining.

If that doesn't work, hold the leash in one hand and place your other hand on his rump. Very gently, apply pressure and issue the command again. Once he can completely sit, wait three seconds and then back up a few feet as you call him to you and praise him. Then lead him back to his spot and start over. If your dog gets up and breaks his position the minute he sits or when you show him a treat, very gently lead him back to the spot with his leash and tell him to sit again.

If you're not perfect at the commands and getting him to comply is proving to be a struggle, do whatever you need to do to get him to sit. Just be sure to do it gently and consistently, and praise him for it when he succeeds. When it comes down to it, you want to make it fun for both of you.

After the first week of training, he'll fully understand what the word "sit" means, so be sure not to continuously repeat your commands after that first week. You don't want to inadvertently teach him that he doesn't need to comply on the first command. Issue the command once, and if he doesn't comply, enforce it by gently applying pressure on his rump and asking him to sit.

Always keep a smile on your face—he'll be less inclined to comply if he thinks he's in trouble. Don't forget to praise him when he follows your command by saying "Good sit!" In time, he will master the command and respond off-lead. Practice this routine three times a day for 10 minutes each session, and you'll have a savvy sitter in no time!

Down

The next command is *down*. First, make eye contact and tell your dog to sit. Remember to always use a happy tone of voice, as training is supposed be fun! Then, show him a treat. This should be a special treat that he gets only during training. Because the down command is the most submissive position for your dog, you'll want to use something really yummy! (The only way I got my overly active toddler to sit was to bribe him with French fries and a strawberry shake. Although I'm sure Fido would do cartwheels for that, I advise you not to give him canine junk food—use something healthy, such as the treats noted in chapter one.)

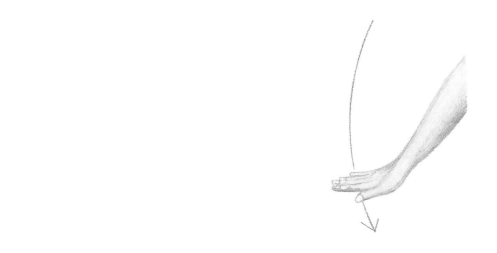

When teaching your dog the down command, always gesture toward the floor so he understands exactly where you want him to be.

Hold the treat in the hand you use to point to the floor in front of him, and keep it there while issuing the command "down" until his body is on the floor. Generally, your dog will lie down easily this way, because it will be the only way he can get to the treat—especially if you feed it to him once he's down.

A treat-free approach to the down command is to make your dog sit, issue the down command, then gently pull his legs out in front of him; this forces his tummy toward the floor. Use this same technique if he resists compliance. Once he is lying down, praise him in an excited way with "Good down!" Being enthusiastic about this particular command is very important, because it's the most submissive position for a dog, and you don't want him to feel as if he's being punished during training.

The down command can be confusing to your dog if not issued properly. People often get the down command confused with the *off* command. The down command is for getting your dog to lie down; the off command is to stop him from imposing his body on a person, place, or object.

Practice the down command three times a day, for 10 minutes each session, and you'll have a dynamite downer in no time!

Say "off" when asking your dog to remove his body from the furniture, not "down."

Stay

Begin teaching the stay command on-leash, so you have total control of your dog. The most effective way to start teaching stay is to put your dog into the "down" position. This can be done by either starting your dog from a sitting position and gently pulling his front legs outward until his belly touches the floor, or showing him a motivator such as a treat or toy. Place the motivator on the ground in front of him (continuing to hold it yourself), until he lies down on his own. Once down, withdraw the motivator and put your hand in front of his face as the illustration depicts, while firmly saying "stay", backing up to the length of the leash without pulling it tight.

A good rule of thumb is not to repeat your commands, but issue the command only once. If the command is ignored or broken (as you can expect when a dog is just learning a command) say "no" firmly and gently lead him back to the original training spot. Bring him back into a down position and issue "stay" only once. Make sure your that you only keep him in a stay command for a count of five or ten seconds so that he may experience praise from you for

staying, thus encouraging him to do better next time. Once he has completed your command, smile and say, "ok, you're free!" gently tugging on the leash and offering him the motivator. Remember that your kisses and hugs are his true praise and make sure you offer that last, as to not mislead him into thinking that the food or toy is his reward.

Repeat the steps above, training three times a day for 10 minutes each session and you'll have a solid stayer in no time! You can then graduate to a longer leash each month, until he can successfully master his "stay" at 100 feet (30.5 m). This will help you to teach him stay off-leash—at the front door when a guest arrives, for example, or if he gets loose by mistake.

Practice makes perfect—10 minutes a day will make a solid stayer.

Come

The next technique to practice is the recall command or come. (You can also use "come here!" if you are more comfortable with this command.) Come is the second part of the stay session. Once you have taught your dog to stay, stand in front of him, as far back as the length of the leash will allow, and with a smile and happy tone, say "Come here," while gently pulling on the leash to guide him toward you. Once he has complied with the command, make him sit, give him a treat, and issue a "Good dog!" He will be so thrilled to see how happy you are that he'll want to do it over and over again! If he doesn't comply, you will need to physically retrieve your dog and bring him to you.

If your dog is not motivated by treats, use a favorite ball or toy as a focal point during training sessions, making sure to play with him after each session.

When you're done with the training sessions, say, "You're free!" This lets your dog know that he can now relax, play, and no longer needs to focus. Just as in the stay command, in order to graduate from a standard on-leash recall to off-leash recall ability, start with a 25 foot (7.6 m) lead and work up to 100 feet (30.5 m). Once that distance has been mastered, your dog should comply with the recall command by voice alone. Remember: Patience, consistency, and praise during training are the three keys to having a well-behaved and happy dog.

TRAINING REMINDERS

- Treats and toys are not rewards but motivators—your love and praise are the true rewards!

- Be patient.

- Be consistent.

- Use eye contact as much as possible.

- Think about being the dog: How would you want to be treated?

- Focus on the tone of your voice—sound happy!

LOUIE'S STORY

Meg's Chihuahua thought he was Attila the Hun. Louie growled at other dogs, people, and kids whenever they came close to Meg. He even growled at her when she moved around too much in bed or walked too close to him when he was napping. One day, Louie got hold of a chicken bone she accidentally dropped on the floor, and, when Meg attempted retrieval, Louie nipped her, not hard enough to break the skin, but enough to leave a mark on her hand—and her heart.

Meg worried that without professional help, she would need a crucifix and some holy water! So she called me. I told her that I no longer perform dog-exorcisms, but would be happy to give her some sound advice.

When I came in the door, Louie wanted to pull my eyelashes out one by one. He was not happy that I, a stranger, had dared step foot in his domain. He challenged me over and over again, darting at my feet and ankles, like he was trying to take down a giraffe. I watched Meg turn red and withdraw from the whole situation. I could see that she had no control over Louie and that he had no respect for her.

I had Meg put Louie in the bathroom and close the door, so we could talk without being cussed at in several different dog languages. After talking a while, Meg agreed that Louie was the Alpha and wore the pants in the family. But she was ready to start fresh and gain some badly needed control.

I told her to enroll Louie in obedience classes. The classes would give Meg the confidence she needed to handle him properly in the presence of others. I also gave her an "order": Louie was no longer allowed to sleep in bed with her until he had learned to behave. A dog that growls at his human for moving around in bed should not be tolerated. It was time for Louie to have his own sleeping space in a crate. I also suggested that when he growled at Meg for disturbing his napping space, she squirt him with water and tell him firmly, "No growl!" When he stopped, she should praise him.

Next, Meg was to make him sit before walks, play, and food. I suggested she keep him on a leash for a while, to enforce the command if need be, until he got used to the new doggy boot camp. I told her it was imperative that she stop carrying him everywhere and make him walk on-leash, unless there were big, unleashed dogs around. Carrying him everywhere and holding him close gave him the message that she needed protection—the result being that he growled when anyone approached.

Finally, she was to keep him leashed when guests visited, and if he continued barking and growling during the visit, she was to put him in his crate in the bedroom and close the door. I told her to leave him out every week when a guest came over, until he acted up, and at that point she was to put him in time-out until she could see that the isolation training was working.

It took some time, and Meg often felt like she was being mean to her dog. But when Louie's behavior improved after a couple weeks, she really gave it her all. She called me six months later, to tell me how much things had changed for the better. The program didn't turn Louie into Lassie, but it did fix the behavior. Three years later, Louie still has not growled or nipped at her or anyone else. Meg is sleeping much better and has guests over regularly, and the only things she carries now are a purse and poop bags!

Speaking Dog

THE NUMBER ONE COMPLAINT I HEAR FROM MY clients is that their dogs refuse to listen, despite knowing exactly what the commands mean. The owner ends up repeating the command over and over, while the dog refuses to comply. You swear he's thinking: "So, let me get this straight. You've told me eleven times to stop sniffing the buffet, and this is supposed to affect me, how?"

Repeating your commands is akin to a parent's "empty threat." (How many times will kids test your patience or not clean their rooms if they aren't forced to?) If you want your dog to take you seriously and obey you the first time, don't repeat commands.

Don't get so upset at your pooch for not listening that you start yelling and making yourself even angrier. Speak clearly and concisely when giving commands, using no more than two to three words at a time, and always use eye contact. Like us, dogs communicate with their eyes. By using eye contact and only one command, you are expressing leadership.

To be successful at speaking dog, you must live by the motto, "Never give a command that you can't enforce". You will never convince your dog that you're serious if you're staring at the ceiling or the ground, or waving your arms around, shouting, begging, or bargaining with him to comply; you're only proving you have no power over him. By using eye contact and only one command, you express leadership.

Remember to enforce a command when your dog won't comply. This shows him that you'll back up your words and that he will not get his way. (Ancient Dog Training Secret: this works wonders for kids and spouses, too!)

Sometimes we confuse our dogs by giving them mixed signals. You feed your dog at the dinner table and then expect him not to beg at your dinner party. You let him sleep on the sofa but get angry when you find him on the bed. Be consistent with your approach to discipline. You need to decide if you want your dog to bark at everyone or no one. It's unfair to expect him to know that you need him to bite the burglar but kiss the mailman. Dogs are intuitive, but they can't read your mind.

You must also be consistent with how and when you issue commands. For example, if you don't like your dog lying on the sofa, you must issue the off command every time you catch him there. If, once or twice a week, you decide that you're too tired to deal with it and let him stay there, you'll confuse him the next time you demand that he get off. He doesn't understand why some days, you yell at him for it, and other days, you don't.

Over time, confusion leads to behavior problems. If you have problems with your dog, perhaps it's time to assess your relationship with him. Ask yourself if it's possible that you're giving him mixed signals. Do you discipline your dog by your mood? For example, do you get angry at your dog for sleeping on the bed when you're in a foul mood, but when you're happy, it's no big deal? Do you laugh when your dog exhibits a certain behavior but at other times yell at him for it? No one is a perfect—we have all done this once or twice. Be aware of your actions, and try to put more effort into catching the traps you may set for your dog. Being conscious of your own behavior can lead to a happier and more fulfilling life for both you and your dog.

HOW TO SPEAK DOG

- Do not repeat commands.
- Use 2- to 3-word commands only.
- Use eye contact.
- Enforce your commands with consistent discipline.
- Use a "time-out" area for discipline (*see* chapter five for more on this).

Just like you, your dog needs to know he's loved and that you're happy with the good things he does.

Love and Praise

LOVE AND PRAISE ARE EXTREMELY IMPORTANT AND useful tools in training. Petting your dog and using words of love and encouragement whenever he complies with a command or does something that makes you happy encourages him to seek out this response as often as possible and be a better dog. Make training fun for your dog by showing appreciation and love.

Consider how you would feel if someone you loved never complimented you or said anything to make you feel you were important in his or her life. Chances are, you'd suffer from low self-esteem or possibly even behavioral problems. The same thing applies to your dog. He needs to know what makes you happy.

Dogs often think that exhibiting certain behaviors makes us happy, when in reality, they often are just annoying us. You need to let your dog know, gently and consistently, when a behavior is unacceptable, then praise him when he complies. Take, for example, a dog who likes to lick your face. He does it out of respect and submission, not to annoy you. If you get angry with him, he may feel ashamed and insecure. A better response is to use love and praise: gently push him back and say "No lick." When he can greet you without licking you, praise him and say "Good dog!" It won't take him long to learn what makes you happy when greeting you. Rewarding your dog with love and praise every time he complies with a command keeps your dog from becoming confused and making mistakes. For example, if you stop on the street to talk to a friend and tell your dog to sit, praise him when he complies. Forgetting to praise him or ignoring Fido altogether confuses him—in no time, he's not sitting and is distracting you by pulling on the leash. He did what you wanted but got no response from you. This makes it difficult for him to know what

he should do and what makes you happy. Pay attention to your words and follow up the sit command with stay. Then say "Good boy . . . good sit" or "Good stay," and go on with your conversation.

Dogs can frustrate you, but when you react with anger, you create a fear-based relationship, which stresses the dog and creates more behavioral issues. It becomes a vicious cycle. For example: You get angry with your dog because he wants to play and you don't. He's nudging your hand with his nose while you're piecing together a report for work. You continue to ignore him. He's getting a little hyper and has now started to whine. In a moment of intolerance that clearly identifies to him that you're not happy, you respond by perhaps swatting his rump or shouting "Go lie down!" Your response expresses to the dog that he has done something wrong by showing you affection and attention and does not foster a healthy relationship between the two of you.

Many people complain that when their dog complies and they praise him in return, he interprets the praise as an invitation to play, becoming excited and exhibiting the same poor behavior all over again. This does happen. This is why you need to use patience, repetition, and consistency to gain control over the dog. Just as we don't learn a new language in a day, a dog needs some time to learn what is expected of him, especially if this is a dog that has not been with you since puppyhood.

Dogs from shelters, for instance, have often been mistreated and do not begin to trust their new home for at least three to six months, depending on what kind of trauma they survived. Others may have been trained or taught in a different way than the approach you're using. Commands might have been spoken in another language, and you would have no way to know that. Keep these things in mind if your dog has come to you later in his life and he does not comply with you right away. He simply may not understand the commands you are issuing.

Be patient and consistent, and you will see results. Like people, some dogs take a little bit longer than others to catch on. Consider your dog's personality, age, and breed when starting training. If he is particularly hyper, it can take him longer to learn. Without love and praise, it will take him twice as long and won't be nearly half as fun!

SOME POPULAR DOG NAMES

Baby	Misty
Bandit	Molly
Bear	Muffin
Bo	Patches
Brandy	Pepper
Buddy	Princess
Buster	Rocky
Charlie	Rusty
Ginger	Sam
Jake	Samantha
Lady	Shadow
Lucky	Sheba
Maggie	Smokey
Max	Tiger
Missy	Tigger

Chapter Three

The Urinators

. . . and Other Elimination Issues

Potty troubles with your pooch can leave even the most patient person feeling frustrated and reconsidering whether to own a dog at all. The thoughts you once had about bringing home a cute little puppy have now faded into the subject of how to artistically apply plastic wrap to her bottom so your carpet can take a break! Rest assured, you are not the only new-dog owner to feel this way.

Until your puppy is sixteen weeks of age, it's common for accidents to occur during the housebreaking process. If, however, your puppy reaches five or six months old and is still having accidents, it's time to take action.

Peeing Inside

FIRST AND MOST IMPORTANT TO REMEMBER ABOUT urinary problems is that it is not your dog's fault; she does not pee in the house to "get back at you" for something she is unhappy about. I can't tell you how many times, in my career as a dog trainer, I have heard dog owners express the opinion that his or her dog is getting "revenge" or "doing it on purpose." Dogs don't harbor malicious thoughts of revenge or look for ways to get back at you for leaving them alone or not giving them a piece of your steak. They are simple creatures and require few things to keep them happy. Failing to score a piece of last night's London broil will not be the reason Fido ruins your newly installed Berber carpet today.

Dogs exhibit potty troubles for many reasons: stress, emotional issues, intolerance of inclement weather, separation anxiety, and physical issues such as age-related disorders, bladder disease, and urinary infections, stones, or defects. Becoming angry with your dog for peeing where she shouldn't only makes the problem worse. Your anger just frightens her and makes her likely to lose control of her bladder again. It also makes her fearful about going potty, which compounds the problem, because she'll learn to hide it from you by peeing under a table or behind a piece of furniture.

Your dog has only a 10- to 20-second memory of everything she does. She'll remember places, people, food, and toys she likes, but she won't remember what she did 20 seconds ago. Rubbing your dog's nose or face into a spot you find 30 minutes after she made it only confuses her, because she has absolutely no clue why you are angry. Urinating is a natural bodily function. Making your dog feel terrified to do what comes naturally can be damaging to your dog—and to your relationship with her, by ruining the trust and bond between you.

Until you can change your dog's behavior, you need to simply clean up any spots you find and let it go. Yelling, spanking, or worse, shoving her face into the carpet is abusive treatment and is very unfair to your dog.

It's possible that your dog's problem isn't behavioral but physical. Assuming that potty issues are completely behavior-related can lead to delaying medical consultation, committing the dog to an outdoor life, and even euthanasia. However, urinary incontinence is usually one of easiest problems to solve, so it is crucial that dog owners seek assistance and counsel from their veterinarian before their patience runs out and any permanent decisions are made about the dog and her future in the home.

Your veterinarian's office is the first place to go to rule out any possible urinary medical conditions before starting a behavior program.

Ruling Out Physical Problems

Before beginning a potty-training program, rule out any medical conditions that might be causing the behavior. It's possible that your dog may have a urinary tract infection (UTI) or bladder disease, often referred to as urolithiasis, cystitis, urethritis, urinary calculi, and bladder stones.

If your dog has peed minimally in several spots and seems to circle the room frequently, sniffing for a spot to eliminate, she could have an infection. If you suspect your dog of having a UTI, call your vet to schedule an exam. Female dogs seem to be more susceptible than male dogs to UTIs, but the infection can affect both sexes. It's difficult to detect in males because they mark their territory, eliminating on every tree and bush along the walk, making it difficult to determine whether they have a UTI or are just expressing normal marking. An untreated UTI can turn into a more serious problem if the infection spreads to the kidneys. Be sure to have a canine urinalysis done to ensure you don't wind up with a very sick puppy.

Once a UTI or bladder disease has been ruled out, look into whether or not your dog has incontinence or a weak bladder. Certain dogs can't retain urine in their bladder when they sleep, and many suffer from incontinence as they age; the muscles controlling the bladder become weak. In female dogs, hormones play a role in elimination, and spaying can cause hormone-responsive incontinence. Practitioners of Chinese medicine also suggest that spay surgery disrupts an energy meridian along the front midline of the dog's body (the "conception vessel," or CV) and creates an energy blockage, which contributes to incontinence.

If your pooch is diagnosed with a weak bladder, your vet may recommend medicine or a procedure to fix it. However, puppy diapers are your best bet when she is left alone. If your vet gives your dog a clean bill of health, you will know the problem is behavioral.

Make sure that you start out on a positive note with a puppy by praising her when she eliminates properly. This will help her to avoid feelings of "Potty Fear" in the future, which may cause potty problems in the house.

- Stop feeding wet food indefinitely, as it contains high amounts of water. However, never keep water away from your dog; it could cause dehydration, which can be deadly.

- Avoid giving your dog people food, especially food that's high in sodium.

- Avoid dog food with chemical preservatives that may irritate the bladder.

- Walk your dog right before bed to reduce the chance of an accident during the night.

The Potty Problems Program

You'll want to prepare a few things before starting my Potty Problems Program (PPP), to help ensure total success:

2 or 3 bottles of a brand name enzymatic urine and odor eliminator (buy the "pour" bottle, rather than the spray)

black light urine detector, found at a local pet, hardware, or home store

75-foot (23 m) extension cord attached to the light, for scanning larger rooms

ball of twine

pair of small scissors

The smell of urine triggers a dog's need to urinate, so before you can eliminate the behavior, you will have to eliminate the urine already in the carpet. Start by using a baby gate to keep her out of carpeted rooms and/or confine her to a "safe room" with a vinyl or wood floor until she is trained. This could be the bathroom, laundry, or even the kitchen. Put down absorbent wee-wee pads, found at your local pet store. If you don't have *any* uncarpeted rooms, pull up the carpet in one room altogether, or keep your dog confined outside when you cannot watch her completely. If possible, board your dog for a few days during the cleaning process.

When evening falls, turn off the lights and run the black light closely over the carpet in each room of the house. Because it contains phosphorous, dog urine will fluoresce under the black light. Once you locate each spot, mark its circumference with a piece of cut twine, so you can clearly see the spot when the lights are back on. Be careful in the darkness not to disturb the outlines by stepping on them. Next, saturate twice the size of the circumference of the spot with the urine eliminator, and let it soak for at least 20 minutes. Much of the urine is absorbed by the padding beneath the carpet, so spraying the top of the carpet does not eliminate it—and if the dog can still smell it, she will continue to use the spot for potty visits. Soak up the excess product with an absorbent cloth or terry cloth towel, and allow the carpet to dry fully before allowing your dog back into that area. If you have or can rent a steam cleaner, mix one quarter of the eliminator product to three quarters water and clean the entire carpet in each room, to give additional protection and deodorization.

Once you have cleaned the carpet, you will need to keep her with you on-leash as much as possible. This will prevent her from sneaking off and peeing when your back is turned or you're not nearby. Attach the dog to your belt, wrist, or a piece of furniture. If you will be sitting for longer than 30 minutes, make sure you have a wee-wee pad at your feet, in case she needs to go. Give her plenty of toys and chew items to keep her busy, and when she can't be with you—or when you've had enough—put her back into the safe room.

Stay vigilant about watching her. Even two weeks without potty accidents does not mean you're in the clear. That will come when your dog has mastered the art of going outside and leaving the carpet alone for six weeks.

Potty Breaks

The next part of the regimen is to buy a special "potty" treat—something yummy and irresistible that she only gets when going outside to pee. It might not be fun to take your dog out ten times a day, especially if the weather is nasty, but it's important to do it anyway, because she needs as many potty opportunities as possible to keep her from peeing in the house. You will spend much less time taking her outside than you will spend on your hands and knees cleaning urine spots out of the carpet. You'll find it's worth the effort when you come back to a clean-smelling, pee-free home!

Whenever you take your dog out, practice teaching her to go potty "on command." Find your dog's favorite "pee spot." While she attempts to pee, repeat over and over, "Go potty." Do not show her the special treat until she finally goes. After a few runs, she may catch on that you have treats in your pocket, but she'll soon realize that, to get one, she's got to produce!

If, after your best effort, your dog won't pee outside and you've caught her in the act or within 10 seconds of peeing in the house, say firmly, "No! Potty outside." Put a leash on her immediately and take her outside, leading her to the "pee spot." Follow the instructions above, giving the command in a friendly tone. Give your dog 5 to 10 minutes to pee (weather permitting of course), and if she doesn't go, try again later.

When she finally goes potty outside, praise her with much exuberance—the kind that will make your neighbors think you've just seen Elvis. Make a huge deal about it and offer her a special treat. If your dog isn't food-motivated, throw a favorite ball for her, or give her a toy reserved only for potty times. Once she associates going potty outside with a positive, fun experience, she will want that experience again and will soon learn how to achieve it.

For tough cases, try leaving urine-soaked housebreaking pads outside on the pee spot, to help trigger the urgency to go. Remove them as soon as she goes pee outside on her own, so she doesn't become familiar with the pads always being outside.

At night, it's wise to crate your dog or put her in the safe room. If she's used to sleeping in your room or on your bed and has never had issues peeing there, it should be okay to continue that, as long as you close the door to prevent her from going out into the living room or den to pee in the wee hours.

If you are confining your dog to a crate at night for the first time, give her a big stuffed animal to cuddle up to and a chew treat to keep her busy. If she will not be in your bedroom, close to you, I also suggest leaving the radio or TV on low, to ease her anxiety about being separated from you and to cover any outside noise that could cause her to feel anxious and trapped.

Once you have completely eliminated the odor in your carpets and followed the PPP, you will encounter another kind of PPP: Peace, Pleasure, and Paradise!

MORE WAYS TO DEAL WITH POTTY PROBLEMS

- Put a puppy diaper on your pooch when you're home and can't watch her, but give her freedom to roam the house. To prevent her from chewing off pieces of her diaper and swallowing them, use a canvas diaper cover with Velcro tabs, which can be found in most local pet stores. Depending on the size of your dog, these might need to be purchased via the Internet (see Resources, page 170).

- Hire a dog walker to come in several times a day and walk her when you are away from home.

- Send her daily to doggy day care, so she's only at home when you are.

- Confine your dog to a crate during the day—but for no more than five hours.

Marking Territory

DOES YOUR DOG NEED TO MARK EVERY FOOT OF your walk together? Does he mark in the house or on your objects, clothing, or furniture? Although male and female dogs both mark their territories, it's more common in males. By peeing on a spot, they are saying, "This my space—I own it, so back off!"

Dogs mark objects to communicate with others of their kind. It serves as a calling card and offers information such as sex and reproductive status. Dogs also mark their territory to avoid confrontation. How much they mark has a lot to do with the environment and how comfortable they feel. For instance, if a dog is insecure about its surround-

ings, he will mark his territory more frequently. Any object is at risk: beds, clothing, even visitors. Dogs also urinate over another dog's marking to say, "Hey! I was here!"

Marking in the house is common if another dog comes to visit and the resident dog feels the need to reinforce who is really king of the castle. The visiting dog may feel the need to mark due to being insecure in unfamiliar surroundings, which triggers the resident to respond with, "Oh no, you don't! If any marking is going to be done on my turf, it's gonna be by me!" as he marks over the other dog's pee. And round and round we go.

You cannot prevent your dog from marking on an outdoor walk—and, frankly, asking that of him is unfair and unnatural—but you can and should expect it to end there. At home, *you* are the king of the castle, and you must discipline this bad habit as soon as it starts.

If you find that other dogs trigger this behavior, ask your friends to keep their dogs at home, if possible. An alternative is to put the visiting dog in the backyard or garage. If you must allow the other dog into your home, make sure the encounter with your dog is friendly, and keep them confined in a "safe room." Watch your dog closely for signs of marking, so you can properly discipline him by saying firmly, "No marking!" Then take him outside, into the safe room, or to the garage.

Remember not to get angry with your dog for marking. He has as much right to protect his terri-

Many submissive dogs will pee and then roll over. Scolding or reprimanding your dog during submissive peeing will only make the problem worse and impossible to solve. Keep greetings upon your arrival calm and wait until he has settled down before giving him your full attention.

tory from other dogs as you do to protect your house from intruders. Shaking an aluminum can filled with a few coins in his face will help to establish your displeasure when he marks. Then take him immediately outside or into the safe room. Follow the cleaning techniques given on page 80 to eliminate odor and urine from the carpet. You can also use the urine elimination product on cloth furniture by saturating the spot. On wood and other nonporous surfaces, spray with the product, and wipe clean.

- Greet your dog in a nonexcited, casual way when entering the home, and don't pay too much attention to her.

- Never lean or tower over your dog when greeting her. This can be very intimidating. Rather, crouch down and pet her chest, instead of the top of her head.

- Avoid prolonged eye contact, as this is also intimidating. Look around, just glancing at her while interacting.

- Distract her from her submissiveness. Throw her a toy or a ball when you walk through the door.

- Always use a calm, happy tone of voice.

Peeing on People

DOGS PEE ON PEOPLE FOR SEVERAL REASONS. FOR one, this claims someone they like and want to "keep." Marking the person discourages other dogs from attempting to stake their own claim. Younger dogs can pee from excitement at playtime invitations or during greetings, especially if you've been absent for a long time. Generally, if you keep greetings low-key, your dog will grow out of it.

Dogs may also pee to express submission. This generally occurs when a younger dog feels insecure, frightened, or threatened. Shelter dogs that have been abused tend to submissively pee when they are being shown affection, because they are desperate for approval and feel the need to show their respect.

Submissive peeing can also occur when your dog is being disciplined and she senses your unhappiness, or when she's approached by someone she finds strange or frightening. You can help your dog overcome this with confidence-building tactics, such as obedience training and dog agility, where your dog can have fun, succeed in a job, and become desensitized to other people on a regular basis. You can also play fun and simple games in which you let the dog win and then praise her for it. The longer she is with you, the more she will trust you and the less insecure she'll become.

To help save your floors, invite your dog to come out to the porch to greet you, so urine won't ruin your entryway. At the entry, put down an absorbent rug that can be safely soiled and then thrown into the wash.

DEALING WITH LAWN BURNS

The best way to avoid lawn burns is to run outside and pick up feces right away or spray the urine-soaked grass with the hose after every tinkle. But this isn't always practical. You can reduce the lawn damage, however, by training your dog to go in a specific area and by changing your dog's diet to reduce the amount of nitrogen expelled in the urine and feces. The excessive nitrogen is what burns the lawn.

Nitrogen is produced when protein is broken down during the digestive process. What isn't used by the body is excreted during urination. All carnivores, including dogs, have significant protein requirements, and urine volume and production varies with their size and metabolism. Obviously, bigger dogs will produce more urine, but some small dogs have higher metabolisms and drink copious amounts of water, making them more of a culprit for burning the lawn than other small dogs. Feces are less of a problem—they tend to "fertilize" the grass over time—but urine can act as a concentrated liquid fertilizer.

Female dogs generally squat to urinate, and are more likely to cause lawn damage. Unlike male dogs, which lift their legs at about a year old and urinate on a tree or other plant, female dogs empty their bladders all at once—usually on the lawn. The result is a large nitrogen dump confined to a small patch of grass. This leaves a brown spot, with a green ring toward the outer edge.

You can reduce the nitrogen concentration in urine by changing your dog's diet. Switch to an all-natural food without chemical preservatives. There are natural foods containing a higher-quality grade of protein that is easier for dogs to digest.

Wet food combined with dry is better than dry alone; dry food contains more protein, and wet food has more water, which dilutes the urine. The more diluted the urine is, the less possibility of serious lawn burns. If you choose to give dry food only, wet it with water and exercise your dog more to increase her thirst and make her drink more water. The average family dog doesn't get enough exercise to warrant the high protein content that most commercial dog foods provide. Increasing your dog's water intake through additional exercise can help a lot.

To help reduce the lawn damage, contain the dog by tie-line or a kennel in an area of lawn you don't care about. You can also train her to go in a certain spot by keeping her on a leash during potty breaks and using treats and praise to let her know you are happy with where she is going potty. Removing all feces from other areas and putting it in the new spot helps the dog understand that this is the "potty place." It can take two to three weeks to train the dog this way.

If you find that these methods are not working for you, it may be less expensive to get help from a professional dog trainer than it would be to reseed your lawn.

Poop Eating (*Coprophagia*)

MOST DOGS, AT SOME POINT, WILL BE TEMPTED TO taste another's waste!

Poop eating, or *coprophagia*, can be very embarrassing for you if your dog is prone to this. However, you are not the only dog owner looking over your shoulder, nor are you to blame for your dog's perverse cravings. The canine palate is very different from ours. Dogs can smell many more things than we can imagine. To us, a dog's elimination is just that—something to get rid of. However, some dogs find feces appealing.

There are several different categories of *coprophagia*: autocoprophagia (when a dog eats its own feces); *intraspecific coprophagia* (dog eating another dog's feces); and *interspecific coprophagia* (dog eating feces from another species, such as cat or deer).

Coprophagia can be caused by physical problems, such as exocrine pancreatic insufficiency, pancreatitis, intestinal infections, malabsorptive syndromes, and overfeeding. It can also be behavioral. Behavioral reasons why a dog will eat feces include:

- **Attention-seeking behavior. In times of stress or boredom, your dog may have learned that this behavior receives a reaction from you. When she can't get positive attention from you, she will seek out negative attention as a consolation.**
- **Observance or *allelomimetic* behavior. Your dog watches you pick up and sometimes "keep" poop (not realizing it's just until you can find a trash can), so she copies the behavior, perhaps thinking that, because you like to do it, it may please you! Her mouth is akin to our hands.**
- **Parental behavior. A mother dog with pups will often eat feces to keep the nursing area clean and, depending on the breed, past history, and whether she is a wild or homeless dog, to prevent the scent of the feces from attracting predators.**
- **Learned behavior. A dog whose siblings exhibit similar behavior will learn it from them. She may also have witnessed other dogs in public, such as at doggy day care or the dog park, eating poop.**
- **Hunger. A dog with constant hunger issues will seek out sources in any form. This is common with dogs that are only fed once a day and remain hungry; they eat animal feces, sometimes their own, as a way to supplement their diet.**

Coprophagia might be embarrassing for you, but it could be hazardous to your dog's health, because she could be ingesting another dog's medications. The best response is to discourage your dog from eating waste. Discipline her the moment she tries it, by issuing a firm command to "Leave it!" while using a shake can containing a few pennies (see page 109) or squirting lemon juice in her mouth with a kid-sized squirt gun. You must give your dog a negative association with the behavior, so she learns that it is not acceptable.

If your dog remains stubbornly interested in her own feces, ask your vet for a special powder, which, when applied to your dog's food, creates an unpleasant taste at the end of the food chain. If you have cats at home, a dog with interspecific *coprophagia* might find their litter gifts too tempting. Make sure you have one litter box for each cat in the home and a good deodorizing litter in the pan. Clean it every time your cat eliminates. If you can't clean it often, buy a self-cleaning litter box or a pan with a top on it and an entrance only large enough to let the cat through. It is also a good idea to put the litter box in an area the dog can't access, such as in a laundry room with a kitty door or in a closet with the door open just enough for your cat, but not the dog, to get in.

You can also sprinkle cayenne pepper on waste in the backyard. Do this every day, and she could become discouraged very quickly. This also helps when you're on walks, because eventually she'll come to think that all poop is too hot for her tastes!

If poop eating only occurs on walks and nowhere else, put a soft nylon muzzle on your dog to prevent her from opening her mouth wide enough to pick anything up. Putting a cage muzzle on her is also a solution. She'll look a bit strange with a cage around her snout, but it's better than having a potty-mouthed pooch! The cage muzzle works well, because it allows her to open her mouth fully to pant or bark but prevents her from eating anything.

Coprophagia is one of the most annoying dog behavior problems on the planet, but it's not impossible to fix. Although it can be very disappointing—and embarrassing—to find that your dog has this habit, you're not alone. I have worked with thousands of clients over the years, and I can confidently say that at least 35 percent of all of my clients' dogs had some interest in all kinds of feces, whether it was smelling it, tasting it, or just rolling in it. Be consistent about prevention and corrective training, and remember, praise is a must. Giving treats is a great way to keep her attention on you and to remind her of what "good food" is all about.

FACE LICKING

I personally don't think it's wise to let your dog lick your face. It is an urban legend that dogs' mouths are cleaner than ours. A dog's mouth harbors many viruses and bacteria— rabies, tetanus, E-coli, and pasteurella, for example— that can infect you. They can also pick up other nasty diseases from partaking in poop eating.

Chapter Four

The Barkers and Destroyers

If I were granted three wishes, I would want one to be that I could communicate with my dog like Dr. Doolittle. It would be very entertaining to banter back and forth with her, to find out what kind of sense of humor she possesses, to know if she likes to be clothed or not, and to learn whether the threads hanging off the tennis ball are of little consequence or if she would prefer a new ball. I would like to ask her if she's ever smelled a rear end she didn't like and if she's really color-blind.

I fear that I'd discover we are *not* the most intelligent species on the planet, that dogs are fully capable of speaking fluent "Doglish" at three months of age, and that they have been cursing us since they started on dry food. I would discover that the annoying licking and chomping sound in the middle of the night has nothing to do with necessity and everything to do with relieving boredom by seeing how long it takes us to crack. I might learn that when dogs pull on the leash, they're not only in a hurry to get to where they're going, they're calling us slow, lazy cows under their breath.

I am not Dr. Doolittle, but I *can* help break the communication barrier between you and your dog—and I can tell you why he barks and how to turn the volume down. Help is on the way. Barking and destructive behavior is not difficult to correct, once you understand why your dog engages in these behaviors.

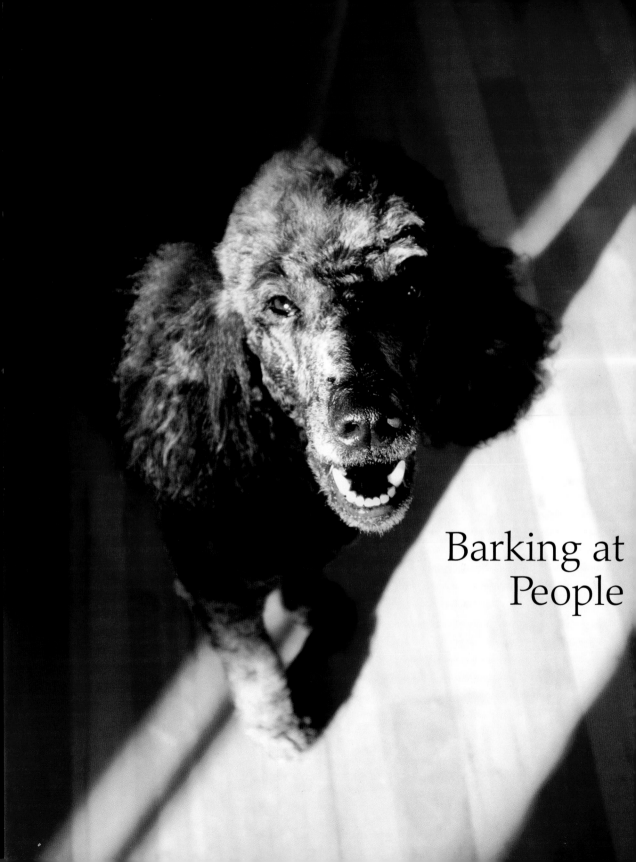

Barking at
People

DOGS BARK AT PEOPLE FOR SEVERAL REASONS. THEY bark at their human (as well as canine) friends to ask for play and attention. They bark to alert their family to the presence of someone outside the home. They bark at strangers to say, "Stay away, this is my territory." And they bark to announce that they're hungry and want food.

If you find it bothersome when your dog barks at you or others, the best reaction is no reaction. The more you respond to his barking with eye contact and verbal response, the more you engage him in a conversation. Leaving the room removes the opportunity for him to communicate with you in an uninvited manner. You could interpret his barking to mean "I want a treat," "I need to go potty," or "Are you still buying me that pony for Christmas?" So, ignore him until he stops, reestablish yourself as the leader by making him sit or lie down, and if it's an appropriate time—and only if he's being quiet—then give him what he's asking for. Be consistent about responding in this way, and he'll soon learn to find more appropriate and quiet ways of getting your attention.

A squirt bottle comes in handy to discourage your dog from barking at guests, especially once they have entered the home. Train your dog to go to a designated area and stay there when you have guests. Keep the squirt bottle handy, in case he decides to leave that area to continue barking at them. Once he's calm and quiet, allow him to share the room with you and your guests. However, the minute he starts barking, squirt him in the face with water, being careful to avoid the eyes, say "No bark!" and send him back to his area.

Dogs bark at people to communicate things like, "I'm hungry!" or "Get off my turf!"

BARKING TO INDICATE DANGER

Your dog may try to get your attention in times of danger by excessively barking. If he seems upset, is running back and forth or in circles while barking, and is not prone to excessive barking (or even if he is), he might be trying to alert you to impending danger, such as a fire or an attempted break-in.

If you suspect that your dog is trying to warn you of danger, assess the situation, and consider calling 911. For safety's sake, don't ignore your dog when he is barking excessively—especially if he does it rarely.

DOG TRIVIA

Royalty favored little dogs for an unusual reason: they put lap dogs under the covers before retiring, so that bedbugs and fleas would jump onto the dog instead of on them.

The Lundehund breed has lived solely on two islands in the north of Norway. Some believe they survived the Ice Age by feeding on sea birds. Lundehund dogs have the coolest feet in dogdom! To seek out its favorite prey, the puffin, from among the rocks, the breed has evolved with several more toes than a normal dog: it has at least two large functional dewclaws and up to eight plantar cushions per foot.

The Lowchen, a breed native to France, is called "petit chien lion," or "little lion dog," because its fur resembles a lion's mane.

The oldest American breed of dog, the American foxhound, dates back to the 1600s.

The gigantic Irish wolfhound is so strong, it can pick up a mastiff by its back and shake it to death. The saluki is depicted in Sumerian carvings that date back to 7,000 BC.

The boxer was named for its manner of fighting; it uses its front paws like a human boxer.

The oldest fossil of a dog, called Hesperocyon, dates back to between 34 and 55 million years ago.

There is recorded proof of a full-grown Chihuahua skeleton that was a total of seven inches in length. Estimates suggest that the weight of the dog couldn't have been more than one pound.

Dalmatians are born solid white.

DNA testing has confirmed that chow chows and Afghan hounds are two of the most ancient dog breeds, the Afghan dating back for many thousands of years.

The oldest British dog breeds are the Cardigan Welsh corgi and the mastiff. The corgi has been traced back to dogs that were brought to Wales by the Celts from the Black Sea around 1,200 BC. The mastiff is descended from the ancient Alaunt and Molosser breeds.

Basenjis, like wolves, do not bark.

The Newfoundland has webbed feet, making it a great swimmer and diver.

Basset hounds cannot swim, because their legs are too short to keep their long, heavy bodies afloat.

To Bark or Not to Bark

Over the years, many clients have told me that they don't like their dogs barking but they *do* want them to deter thieves. This is an unreasonable request. You can't expect your dog to bark only sometimes and not at other times. Your dog doesn't know if the person at the door is your best friend or someone who means to do you harm.

If you want your dog to protect your home by barking when somebody is at the door, be prepared when friends come over, and have the dog secured before they arrive. He may still bark, but at least he won't be barking in your guests' faces. If you need home protection and your dog's barking annoys you, invest in an alarm system.

Dogs that bark together at strangers often start to fight as a result of a "barking competition."

Barking at the TV

DOGS DON'T KNOW THAT WHAT THEY SEE ON TV IS not real. Researchers believe that dogs perceive the television screen to be just another window. Generally, this is indicated by a dog that doesn't bark at "television people" but does bark at "television animals," such as dogs. What your dog is seeing is another dog in his yard or even in his living room, inside a box. His barking doesn't necessarily mean that he is being aggressive or territorial; if your dog enjoys playing with other dogs, he's only barking to get their attention.

You can deter your dog from barking at the TV in several ways. The first approach is to simply remove your dog from the viewing area, so that he is in the same room with you but can't actually see the TV screen. The second approach is to discipline the barking, either with a squirt bottle or a shake can. The third is to arrange more playdates with other dogs, so that when your dog is home, he's tired and isn't triggered to want to play by seeing dogs on TV.

You should discourage barking that is triggered by seeing other animals, such as cats, squirrels, and birds, on TV. This predatory behavior can lead to trouble when it's directed at real-life animals, such as your pet cat or bird. Use strong verbal discipline, combined with the squirt bottle or shake can and removing the dog from the room. Do this consistently, to teach him that when he barks at another animal, he will be disciplined for it, regardless of his intentions.

Puppies will often start a habit of barking at the TV because they don't yet realize that what they see is not "live."

Traumatic Barking

IF A FAMILY MEMBER OR DOG MATE RECENTLY DIED or was re-homed, your dog might be barking out of grief. His barking is a call to the missing to return home. Or, if you live in a quake zone, he might be upset by a recent earthquake and will begin barking at the time of day the quake occurred. It's also possible that he has a medical problem you're unaware of and is barking in response to pain or discomfort. If he's an older dog, he may have had a stroke or developed neurological problems that need to be addressed by your veterinarian as soon as possible.

If you feel that your dog's barking is related to emotional trauma, try distracting him from his barking by petting him, getting up and moving around, taking him for a walk, confining him to a quiet room, or turning up the TV or the radio to drown out the sounds from his exterior environment.

Barking at Noises

OFTEN, WHEN YOUR DOG APPEARS TO BE BARKING at nothing, that nothing is actually something—a noise you cannot hear. Dogs have much better hearing than we do, and their ears are much more mobile than ours. Unlike humans, dogs can adjust their ears to maximize sound reception. Dog ears are supported by muscles that rotate and tilt the ears similar to the movement of a satellite dish. The shape of a dog's ears helps with sound reception, as well. A dog's cupped and curved ears help direct and amplify the sounds he hears, much as cupping our hands around our ears helps us hear better.

Dogs with floppy ears do not hear as well as those with curved ears, because their ears lack the shape and directional ability. But all dogs, floppy-eared or not, can still hear sounds undetectable by the human ear. This is why a human can't hear a high-frequency dog whistle, even though the dog sure can!

Then again, your dog could be barking in response to exterior noises or other dogs barking. How often he barks is directly related to the noise level in your community. Go outside and listen to the sounds of your environment. Your dog might have heard several noises that you didn't. It may help you to understand him better and be less frustrated with his behavior. If your neighborhood is particularly noisy, consider buying a machine that creates white noise or the sound of the ocean to help drown out noisy triggers. These can be found at many home stores.

To discipline all barking behavior, use a squirt bottle filled with water, telling him "No bark!" as you squirt him in the face. Remember to praise him when he stops barking. If he doesn't quiet down, place him in "The Big House" (a crate used for training) covered with a dark blanket for 15 minutes. When he comes out and is being quiet, praise him again. Eventually he'll realize what happens if he doesn't comply. You will soon be on your way to having a well-muffled mutt!

Digging

YOUR DOG LOOKS FORWARD TO HELPING YOU IN the garden. The moment you look away, he'll be unwinding the hose, and helping you get rid of those nasty "weeds" (the pansies you just painstakingly planted).

It's normal for to dogs to dig and generally misbehave in the dirt. Dogs dig for a number of reasons: to have fun, cool off, chase rodents, retrieve bones, escape confinement, or—the best thing—bury that loathsome sweatshirt your husband won't give up. Before you consider replacing your ditch-digging dog with a goldfish, there are a few things you can do to curb his "dirty" behavior.

Providing a homemade sandbox for your "Diggity Dog" can keep your garden from being assaulted!

Digging commonly occurs when pets are left alone without sufficient activity or entertainment. Providing your pooch with fun chew toys, increasing play time and physical activity, and even adopting a second pet from your local animal shelter can do wonders to keep him occupied. Digging in your presence can be controlled by discipline or distraction. Unless you prevent it, the digging will continue in your absence.

TRY THE FOLLOWING
METHODS TO
DISCOURAGE DIGGING:

- Turn on a sprinkler
  or high-powered
  hose and squirt your
  dog as you say "No
  dig!"

- Throw a tin can con-
  taining a few peb-
  bles or pennies in
  his general direction
  as you say "No dig!"

- In a place that he
  seems to target
  often, place chicken
  wire about an inch
  below the top layer
  of soil. Smooth the
  soil, and cover it
  with leaves or
  debris, so he won't
  catch on that you've
  been doing some
  digging yourself!

- Provide an appropri-
  ate digging area by
  building a sandbox.
  Bury dog toys and
  treats in the sand,
  about 3 to 4 inches
  (7.6–10.2 cm) from
  the surface. Revolve
  the toys every other
  day, to prevent
  boredom.

Scratching the Door

IF YOUR DOG IS SECURED IN A DESIGNATED ROOM during the day and is clawing at the door because he wants out, he is likely having separation anxiety or confinement issues. Look ahead to chapter eight to find out how to address separation anxiety issues. Once you've followed the guidelines in that chapter, you'll be ready to prevent the scratching from occurring. The following techniques will help to prevent further damage to the door. Use the one you think will work best for your dog.

- Hang about ten empty soda cans from a fishing line tacked across the bottom quarter of the door, where most of the scratching occurs. When your dog attempts to scratch the door, the cans will be in the way. The sound of the cans clanking together may be just enough to deter him from ever going near the door again.

- Tack two rows of inflated balloons across the bottom of the door, over the scratches. You will need to stay in the room for this. Close the door and wait for him to scratch. When he does, discreetly take a pin and pop a balloon in his face, as if his actions were responsible for the pop. You may need to do this two to three times, but the pop should be enough to frighten him and keep him from scratching at the door. Keep the balloons on the door, fully inflated, for four weeks. This should be long enough to help your dog redirect his boredom and excessive energy and change his behavior for good.

- Use a touch-sensitive training pad, a training device that quickly conditions dogs to avoid off-limits areas and surfaces by emitting a harmless, low-power, electronic stimulus similar to static electricity. Place the device across the lower level of the door, where your dog scratches most. When the device is touched, the battery sends small electric impulses to the mat. These surprising little "zaps" quickly repel most pets, and they generally keep off after only a couple of exposures.

Chewing

CATCHING YOUR DOG IN THE ACT IS THE BEST WAY to handle destructive chewing issues. Yelling at him is not. Many of you have said that your dog *always* knows when he's done something wrong—you can see it in his body language when you approach him. But that is not the case at all. Fido's "guilty" body language is simply a conditioned response to your routine anger and negative demeanor when you come through the door at the end of the day. After a few destructive incidents, you've come to expect something to be chewed up or in disarray when you get home, and he senses this anger in your body language and tone of voice.

Remember your dog's 10-second memory (*see* Peeing Inside, chapter three). He truly has no idea what he did 10 minutes ago. So, unless you catch him in the act of misbehaving, you're only breaking

If your dog is prone to chewing shoes, you need to pay more attention to picking them up.

his spirit and his trust in you when you come home and start yelling after discovering a partially eaten slipper in the bedroom.

All it takes is one heightened emotional incident to set your dog up for a vicious cycle of destruction. It might have been nothing more than a mangled shoe or a magazine, but you overreacted by yelling, rubbing his nose in it, or even spanking him. He didn't understand why you were reacting this way, because it happened thirty minutes after you left in the morning. By five o'clock in the evening he had forgotten all about it and as usual, lay waiting in happy anticipation for your arrival. He got the Big

HELPFUL TIPS FOR ALL DESTRUCTIVE ISSUES

- Don't leave personal belongings or valuable objects lying around for your dog to find. If you don't want it destroyed, don't make it available for destruction.
- "Puppy-proof" your home, using the same methods you would for child-proofing; the objectives for both are almost identical. Crawl around on your hands and knees at your dog's level, to see possible trouble spots you may not have noticed when standing up: wires, coins, and plants, for example.
- Confine your dog to the yard or a safe room, with appropriate chew toys and plenty of fresh water.
- Give your dog plenty of aerobic exercise. Remember that most dogs can walk all day and never get the exercise their bodies truly require. Aerobic exercise includes running or swimming.
- Avoid using "people items" as dog toys. You can't expect your dog to know the difference between his play sock and Daddy's dress sock. This is where the expression "Give a dog a bone" comes in!
- You can't give your dog 100 percent of your attention all the time, so your best friend needs a best friend of his own. If your dog enjoys socializing with others of his kind, get him a pal, or make sure that he has time at the dog park or at doggy day care to make friends and run off some steam.
- When you catch your dog in the act of inappropriate chewing—and *only* when you catch him in the act—use a firm command to "Drop it!" When he complies with your command, praise him with "Good drop it!" and replace the item with an appropriate one. This will teach him the difference between your things and his and that chewing on yours is inappropriate behavior.
- Make sure he gets enough exercise. Remember, ... (I've been saying this for 20 years) ... "A tired dog is a good dog!"

Bad Wolf instead. So now, every time you walk in the door, whether he's done something wrong or not, he's waiting for the doggy-doo to hit the fan.

If more than 10 seconds pass between the time he destroys something and the time you find it, don't punish him—he will not understand what he's done wrong. As hard as it might be, you need to just ignore it and walk away.

Dogs are sensitive creatures. Your dog senses your "wrath," even if you only give him that suspicious eye or ask "What did you do today?" with a slightly suspicious tone. Destructive behavior is a symptom of something your dog is lacking, most likely aerobic activity. I mention this repeatedly throughout the book because it's important to understand that a lack of exercise greatly compromises mood and overall health (and not just your dog's, but yours, too). If your dog is under-exercised and understimulated, he will look for ways to let off steam and have fun. It's your responsibility as a dog owner to provide the right environment for your best friend by making sure he has enough activity in his daily life.

If your dog is prone to destroying things when he's left alone in the house, don't leave him alone without something to keep him busy. If you do, he'll more than likely get in to trouble, and the destruction will ultimately be your fault.

Because your dog's life pretty much revolves around you, he'll experience some level of separation anxiety when you're gone. If not left with toys and treats in a safe, confined area, he'll find enjoyment in your new bamboo footstool. Dogs have no perception of time when you're gone. One hour to you is like a lifetime to your dog.

Before you leave, give your dog plenty of things to play with and chew on—a treat toy filled with all-natural peanut butter, for example, or a big raw bone from the market. Don't forget to leave him plenty of water! Putting up baby gates, or confining him to an area where he can't get into trouble, will do wonders.

Taking your dog on outings, as well as giving him a job to do, can help to prevent boredom at home which leads to destructive behavior.

Chapter Five

The Food Offenders

Most dogs are attracted to food above and beyond any other stimulus This is why it's common practice to use food to teach them a trick or get them to behave. Because we use food so much in day-to-day communication with our dogs, we neglect to realize that, although it is a useful training tool, it can also be a hindrance to establishing proper canine behavior habits.

Many people use food to distract their dog from exhibiting a negative behavior—not listening, for example, or chewing on a favorite pair of shoes. What they're doing, however, is inadvertently rewarding their dog's poor behavior. Occasionally, you need to do whatever you can to distract a dog from injuring itself, even if that means offering a treat to accomplish the task.

The Beggar

THERE ARE SEVERAL WAYS TO ELIMINATE BEGGING behavior. The simplest solution is to keep your dog out of the kitchen during food preparation. (Frankly, if you ask my mother, that goes for kids and husbands as well, and explains my inability to make an edible pie crust.) Allowing your dog into the kitchen makes it hard to resist those big, beckoning brown eyes that say "I'm so deprived! Don't you love me anymore?" Before you know it, you're offering your dog tidbits and initiating bad habits.

The two most effective tools for keeping your dog out of the kitchen are the baby gate and the dog crate. If you already have a crate that your dog uses and enjoys, or at the very least tolerates, buy a different crate for training purposes. Look for a model that differs from what you have now, so it has an unfamiliar feel and will not be associated with the existing happy crate; you don't want to discourage your dog from using that one. The crate used for training is called "The Big House."

You will also need a new dog bed and a dark blanket as a part of your training tools. You do not want to use beds and kennels with which your dog has a positive association. The bed and dark blanket should be placed in a designated area that will become "The Hangout." Finally, you will need a few empty soda cans, some duct tape, a handful of pennies, and a clean squirt bottle.

Training Techniques for Begging

The training tool you choose may depend on your dog's personality. You should also feel comfortable using the technique. There are several options:

The Can-Can

STEP 1. *Drop a handful of pennies into a soda can and tape the top closed with duct tape. I recommend soda cans because they make more noise than other cans. For quick access, keep them near various eating areas in your home. They can even be covered with a decorative fabric to blend in better with your décor.*

STEP 2. *When your dog begs, stand up and vigorously shake the can at him while you issue the command "No beg!" Follow with "Go to your hangout!" as you point your finger to the spot where you have placed his dog bed, and then command him to lie down. You may need to keep a leash on your dog to lead him to The Hangout if he is being stubborn (and clearly you will need to work on the down command first, if he doesn't comply). If you have had to lead him on-leash, repeat the word "hangout" as you point your finger, literally touching the dog bed. He will quickly realize what the word "hangout" represents and that this will be where he must stay until he is free.*

1

2

FOR TOUGH, DISCI-
PLINE-RESISTANT DOGS,
instead of shaking,
throw the can of pen-
nies on the floor, just
in front of the dog,
making sure to issue
the commands as you
throw it. Pick it up
immediately after-
wards, so the dog can-
not sniff or familiarize
himself with it.

**TRAINING TERMS
FOR BEGGING**

The Big House

The Hangout

**TRAINING TOOLS FOR
BEGGING**

Dog crate

Baby gate

Dog bed

Dark blanket

Empty soda can

Duct tape

20 to 30 pennies

Squirt bottle

STEP 3. *If, after three attempts, you have failed to control the begging (Three strikes and you're out!),
you will need to give your dog a time-out by
sending him into the The Big House, covered
by a dark blanket, for the remainder of the
meal. Before closing the door, remove from the
crate any toys or treats that he may have
brought in. A leash may be helpful if your dog
is reluctant to enter The Big House.*

STEP 4. *When you have finished dinner, open the door,
and using a light tone of voice, say, "Okay.
You're free!" You don't want your dog to feel
that you're angry once the training session is
completed. However, avoid playing with your
dog or giving him treats for at least twenty minutes after his release. This discourages him
from associating The Big House with a positive
haven.*

*Using confinement can be a simple way to keep your dog from exhibiting negative behav-
iors, especially if you have little time for training.*

The Great Wall

If you have no desire to spend what precious little family mealtime you have
taming the mighty beast, you can always use a baby gate to confine your dog to
the hallway, bathroom, or bedroom. This is a super-easy quick fix, but remember: it doesn't change the behavior, it only prevents it. Once given the opportunity, your dog will beg as enthusiastically as he always has.

Even dogs that like water often dislike being disciplined with it.

Hey, Squirt!

Some dogs are not bothered by the noise a shaken can of pennies makes; they might, however, really dislike getting sprayed in the mug with water. Apply steps 2 through 4 above, replacing the can with a squirt bottle, making sure you aim away from your dog's eyes and focus the stream to the muzzle, the ear, or the rump. You will use the same commands and the same "Three strikes and you're out!" technique.

You will probably have to repeat the can or squirt bottle technique multiple times during each meal of the day, and being constantly interrupted will be frustrating, especially if you're hungry. Remind yourself, when you feel like giving up, that it should only take a few days to gain control over the issue—and a few days of training is easier to endure than years of begging, right?

Make sure you praise your dog every time he complies by using phrases such as "Good down!" or "Good no beg!" Don't be surprised if this makes him playful and he comes back over to you. Just reissue the command to "Go to your hang-out." Quelling the overexcitement of your approval may take a few attempts, but you will quickly see that it just takes picking up the can or squirt bottle to send him running! Use the training tool that works best, so that you can get onto better things, such as having a great relationship with your best friend.

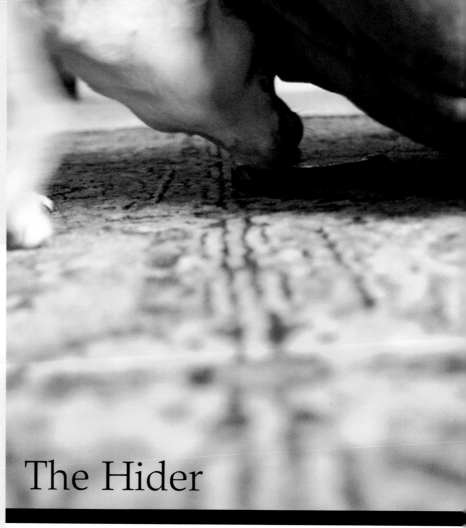

tip

WASH YOUR HANDS THOROUGHLY after handling partially consumed treats of any kind, and *always* wash after touching rawhide, pork skin products, or chew bones made with dehydrated meat.

tip

DON'T ALLOW YOUR DOG to hide or bury treats containing protein for more than thirty minutes; bacteria will start to grow and can be a health hazard, not only to your dog but to you, if your dog licks your face.

The Hider

DOGS HIDE THEIR TREATS BECAUSE IT'S A NATURAL instinct for survival. *You* may not think there is a threat to that soggy, stinky chewy bone, but your dog wants to make sure that all hands are off—especially if you have other dogs in the household. You'll find that if one dog hasn't completely consumed his treat, he will attempt to hide it, to prevent it from being stolen and to enjoy at a later date.

Watch your dog when giving him treats. If you are not keen on finding wet, spongy chew toys under your sofa pillows or bed, contain your dog outside or in a laundry room until the treat has been consumed or enjoyed to capacity. When you find a treat, pick it up, place it in a plastic bag, and refrigerate it for later.

Dogs often hide treats and toys, usually to keep them from other dogs.

112 •

The Thief

PROPERLY STORING FOOD ITEMS—ESPECIALLY ONES that can upset the canine tummy—is the most effective way to deter your dog from stealing food (and ruining your new rug later). To help your dog learn not to steal, you need to discourage him from being in the kitchen or dining areas. If you feed your dog in the kitchen, relocate the food and water bowls to a hallway, mud room, laundry room, or enclosed back porch. A good way to deter your pooch from theft in the kitchen is to use baby gates to prevent him from entering. You also want to make sure that someone is always at the dinner table to discipline him, if the food is left for any length of time.

For the love of food, dogs will do some pretty naughty things when your back is turned!

During parties, either confine your dog or watch him closely, so none of your guests are robbed of their hors d'oeuvres. Be wary of your guests being partners in crime by making the biggest "faux-paw" of all: offering nibbles to your dog. This is a big no-no, and it should be announced to guests once they arrive to "not feed the animals."

The Thievery "Misteak"

The following technique is designed to catch your conniving canine in the act of stealing food, so you can train him not to do it.

Cut a 12-inch (30.5 cm) piece of fishing line or clear thread. Attach a raw steak to one end of the line and six lightweight cooking pots to the other, by slipping the line through the pots' handles or holes. Place the steak on a plastic plate at the edge of the kitchen counter, with pots closely behind, and step aside. Hold the line in the middle, so your dog can't ingest the meat once he's pulled it off the counter. (Holding the line will also ensure the pots fall fast enough.) When Fido grabs the steak off the counter, the pots falling onto the floor will make such a racket that he'll likely drop everything and run away.

Some dogs only need to experience this once; others may need a few times to get the message, but it's a reliable way to solve the problem. Make sure that if you need to set this up a few times for your dog to get the point, you do it consecutively and not allow any thievery in between.

YOU MAY BE CON-CERNED about the pots falling on your dog's body or feet. Generally, he will be far enough away that any risk is minimal. If it does happen, the pots should not be heavy enough to injure him. He may have a pinched toe for a moment, but that's a far cry from hospitalization for ingesting something he shouldn't. A huge amount of money is spent on veterinary care every year, a large percentage of it for stomach pumping and emergency surgeries to correct intestinal blockages from problems caused by food thievery.

TRAINING TOOLS TO CATCH A THIEF

Twine

Extra large sewing needle

Fresh raw steak

6 lightweight cooking pans

1 plastic plate

The Prize Fighter

Depending on who's the Alpha, even little dogs will go after big dogs who try to steal a meal.

FOOD AGGRESSION BETWEEN CANINE SIBLINGS or house guests can occur in the blink of an eye. A fight can injure not just the dogs but you, for trying to break it up. Food aggression is a dominance behavior; a dog acting aggressively is correcting his owner (whom he clearly doesn't see as the leader) or another dog for going near his food. Observe a pack of dogs, wild or domesticated, and you'll see that the Alpha dog always eats first, followed by the subordinate dogs in the hierarchy. If a subordinate dog attempts to eat or sniff the Alpha dog's food, the Alpha will usually let out a warning growl and show his teeth. If the subordinate dog doesn't defer, the Alpha will respond aggressively by biting the offending pack member. This aggressive act reasserts his position as leader and his right to eat first.

If you have two dogs, one of them will be the Alpha of the two, so you should feed him first. However, you should always be Alpha above your dogs and make them sit before you put their food down. This places you in the dominant position and reinforces the message that they depend on you for their survival. As long as they think this way, they will always be more compliant.

The following tips will help keep everyone, including other pets and children, safe during meals:

- **Feed the dog in a separate and quiet place away from the other pets.**

- **Always make the dog sit before you allow him to eat.**

- **Never allow a child to feed a dominant dog or be anywhere near the food bowl, even if it's empty.**

- **If you have multiple dogs, always feed the Alpha dog in the pack first.**

- **Make sure that you place all food bowls far enough apart to allow each dog to feel that he has his own space.**

- **Always pick up the food bowl when the meal is finished and the dog is gone from the area.**

- **Follow these rules for feeding treats as well, and never try to take a bone or treat away from a food-aggressive dog.**

IF YOUR DOG SHOWS AGGRESSION when you try to retrieve a stolen food item, don't attempt to wrestle it from him. Instead, be more diligent in the future about watching the dog when food, especially potentially harmful food, is within his reach. To establish your role as leader and help you gain control over food aggression, always eat before your dog and let him see that you're eating. When you're ready to feed him, make him sit before you put the bowl down. You can reinforce your position by training him not to eat the food in front of him until you give the eat command.

OTHER HELPFUL HINTS FOR THE FOOD GRUMP

- Never offer treats to your dog when other dogs, especially strange dogs from a dog park or beach, are nearby.

- Don't let your dog hang out in places where food might be dropped or offered to your dog without your permission.

- Do not allow a food-aggressive dog around small children who are eating or carrying food.

- Feed a low-carb, high-protein diet, if possible, to curb sugar lows and moodiness due to hunger.

- Avoid feeding your dog people food and snacks.

- Always check with your veterinarian before starting a new diet if your dog has medical problems or is nine years of age or older.

Case Study

BRENDA'S STORY

Sal and Brenda had just sealed their hearts with a wedding. It was a happy time for them, and they wanted to start a family as soon as possible. Both were very active and liked big dogs, so they decided to start their family with two mastiff puppies. Although Sal worked as a fireman and was often gone for 24- to 48-hour shifts, Brenda had a home-based business making gift baskets, so she was able to stay home with "the boys," as she called them.

Life with one puppy is colorful enough, but two proved to be more than Brenda could handle. The pups were getting big—and quickly! They had also become monsters in the kitchen, constantly assaulting her while she was preparing meals, even though they were normally very well behaved. Brenda, who prided herself on the gourmet skills she had learned from her grandmother in Italy, found their behavior very upsetting. The pups were now large enough to jump up and snatch an item off the counter or from her hands, making every meal a nightmare to prepare. The behavior was also potentially dangerous for the dogs, because some foods are toxic to canines. She couldn't lock them out, because her kitchen didn't have a door, but if she relegated them to the backyard, they howled and barked—especially if they smelled food cooking! She knew her neighbors wouldn't tolerate that. Feeling helpless to control the behavior, she called me.

When I arrived, the first thing I noticed was that even though her kitchen had no door, Brenda could easily put up a baby gate to keep out the dogs. While watching the behavior unfold, I also noticed that Brenda didn't give the dogs an alternate source of distraction during kitchen activities, so I recommended that she give each of them a treat toy filled with organic, salt-free peanut butter. Peanut butter is a great source of protein and makes an effective treat, especially when pushed into the holes of a treat toy, because it can take a long time to consume. Its stickiness, combined with the challenge of getting his wide tongue all the way inside the treat toy, will keep a dog busy for some time.

If the dogs became bored with peanut butter, I suggested that Brenda alternate it weekly with organic baby food, such as chicken, beef, turkey, green beans, squash, or carrots. It was food they wanted, so why not give it to them? To make sure this approach did not inadvertently encourage them to produce the negative behavior, I recommended that she give them the treats 15 minutes before she started preparing any meals. Once they were fully involved with the treat, she should put up the baby gate and go about her kitchen business.

Four weeks later, everyone was happy, and the program was working like a charm. However, one day soon after, the largest of the dogs was able to jump the baby gate and bring his treat toy into the kitchen. Although he just seemed to want to be closer to Mom, and he continued with his treat-licking extravaganza, Brenda found this unacceptable. She called me right away and asked what she should do. She was concerned it would become a habit and that the other dog would follow suit. I told her to buy two large plastic crates for the dogs, which would become their hangout during treat time.

She was to place the treats inside first, to encourage the dogs to enter willingly, and, once they were inside, to lock the door behind them. This worked perfectly, and the dogs remained in their crates, sometimes even falling asleep, until she released them. Four years later, they still love their crates *and* their treats, but more importantly, there are a lot of really great meals happening at Brenda's house!

Chapter Six

The Headstrong

Ahhh, the headstrong dog. She's like a bull in a china shop, who leaves the store chasing his ball while licking your leg and sniffing your sandwich.

This chapter is about dogs that just won't listen, comply, or pay attention, a problem made doubly annoying—and even dangerous—because of their strength. I have witnessed dogs literally dragging their owners up to outdoor café tables and swiping food off people's plates. The only good thing about this behavior is finding out that the food, vacuumed up and spat out even more rapidly, is really not as hot as it's cracked up to be!

D-O-G Does Not Spell Horse (Pulling Issues)

MOST UNTRAINED DOGS PULL TO SOME DEGREE, but many have given their people abrasions, sprained wrists and ankles, and even broken bones. Many dogs, despite the general leash-training course, just can't slow down! Here are some tips to help keep your toes—and your dog's—on the ground.

The first step in successful leash training is patience. To dogs, the outside world is filled with invisible fairies and swirling fragrances, causing their every nerve ending to sing as they run. When going for a walk, their mission is to seek out and acquire anything that appeals to the palate and

A dog that pulls is usually under-exercised and needs a good obedience program.

looks or moves even remotely like a ball. On this ride, humans are just the ticket takers.

To help keep your dog focused during training, exercise her for 15 to 30 minutes before you walk her, to release pent-up energy (see chapter one, How Exercise Affects Training, page 37). Bringing along an irresistible treat or favorite toy, if your dog is not food-motivated, also helps to get her attention.

Start your walk by leashing your dog in the house, then make her sit and stay at the front door before you leave. It's crucial that *you* step out of the threshold before your dog does, to establish your position as the Alpha. This not only gives your dog the signal that you're the boss, it also establishes that *you* are taking *her* for a walk and not vice versa! As you walk, let your dog smell, pull, and weave along the way to your destination. This helps her use up some of her anticipatory energy.

On the way back is when you start training. Begin by keeping your dog on the left side of your body. Doing this consistently as you walk together gets your dog used to staying on that side, instead of wandering around you in circles or weaving back and forth. Gently push her to the side with your leg if she continues to cross in front of you.

Carry the treat in your right hand, between your thumb and index finger. Make sure that she sees it, so she focuses on you, wondering when she's going to be rewarded. Engaging her in conversation, talking to her, making silly noises, or whistling also helps to keep her focus. Your neighbors might think you're a bit loopy, but who cares? Your dog will be better trained than theirs!

When starting the leash training, always have your dog sit first and then, in a happy tone of voice, say "Heel!" Keep the leash loose, so she can show you by not pulling that she is listening. If you keep the leash tight, she can't show you what she has learned. The minute she starts to pull, give the heel command again. At the same time, lightly snap the leash like a horse lead, just so she feels the technique but it doesn't hurt or scare her. We only want to redirect her focus toward you.

Once she slows down, give her a big smile and say "Good heel!" Then make her stop and sit, and give her a little treat (or throw a ball). Finish up with a huge dose of love and praise.

If she continues to pull, make her sit repeatedly. Eventually, she will learn that pulling gets her

Playing with your dog before training to let her blow off some steam helps to prevent leash pulling.

nowhere, so she must comply and slow down. Remember to not get frustrated, and always praise your dog when she does a good job. It will help her realize that she is doing exactly what you want her to do. Over time, the good leash behavior will become more evident, until she's well behaved all the time. Don't be impatient—this could take months for her to learn.

Noncompliance

DOG OWNERS REPEAT COMMANDS OVER AND OVER because they don't expect compliance on the first command. Well, why not? Your dog needs to comply with your first command—always. By allowing weak follow-through and by begging or bargaining with her to comply, you are only proving that you have no power over her. If she doesn't comply the first time, you need to *make* her comply, albeit gently. This reinforces your position as leader. For example, if you tell your dog to sit and she doesn't comply, then you need to make her sit by gently pulling up on her collar and pushing down on her rump until she sits on her own. When she does, praise her repeatedly.

An extremely dominant dog might just look at you and think, "Yeah right, whatever, lady." Always have a collar and leash in the house, so that when she refuses, you can take her by the collar and gently make her comply. You don't need to be forceful to be the leader, you just need to be consistent. Remember to live by the motto "Never give a command that you can't enforce."

Help your dog focus during compliance training by using treats or favorite toys to motivate her. You won't need to use these techniques forever—once you teach your dog that you're the leader and you make it fun to listen, she'll comply out of respect, rather than obligation, or to get a treat. Make sure to give your dog lots of love and praise when she complies, even if you don't use a motivator. She may enjoy it even more than a liver snap! A lot of love and little common sense go a long way.

Catch Me if You Can

MORE THAN ANY OTHER COMMAND, "COME HERE" is the most commonly issued—and the most important. It is also the most dangerous for the dog to refuse compliance with, especially if she bolts into the street. Getting angry at your dog, spanking her (a big no-no!), or putting her in "The Big House" when you get her does nothing to encourage her to comply. If your dog doesn't want to come to you, and then is punished when she finally does, why would she want to come the next time she is called? This is exactly why your dog runs even farther away when you try to catch her or yell at her to come. She knows the fun will stop and that you may even smack her or put her in time-out.

Be aware of setting yourself, and your dog, up for failure. For example, if your dog is reluctant to

It's common for young dogs that lack exercise and discipline to challenge you to a "catch me if you can" game when you call them to you.

come when called, letting her roam free in the backyard just before a grooming appointment will only result in frustration and yet another opportunity for your dog to see how little control you have in the relationship. Every time she refuses to comply to a command, you reinforce her perception that she doesn't have to. In this scenario, you've made yourself upset and late for your appointment. Prevention is the key with this game. If you plan on bringing your pooch out and about with you, be conscious of the time, and plan ahead. About an hour before departure, secure her in a confined space with a yummy treat, and she'll be ready to go when it's time to leave.

To help give her good recall skills (coming when called), call her to you several times a day. When she responds, give her a toy or a treat and offer some love and praise. This way, calling her to you won't always represent your departure. You should also never say your dog's name with an angry tone, or punish her for coming to you—as you might be tempted to if she ran out in front of a car. When your dog runs away from you, as difficult as it may be, always smile and sound happy when you call her back; anger and a frown will only drive her farther away.

Think about it. Look at yourself in the mirror with an angry face . . . would you want to come to you? The key is that you want your dog to *always* have a positive association with hearing you call. Also helpful, until she is voice trained, is a tie-line: a steel cable strung between two trees or between a tree and the house. The tie-line, which also has a small cable attached to the collar, gives your dog freedom to roam in the yard but keeps her from retreating when you want to bring her inside. The kit for the line can be found at most local hardware stores. If yours doesn't have it, you can probably buy the components separately. Make sure that your dog has plenty of shade and water when she is on the tie-line for an extended period of time.

COMPLIANCE REMINDERS

- Never give a command you can't enforce.
- Don't repeat your commands.
- If your dog won't listen, "gently" enforce the command.
- Show lots of praise when your dog complies.
- Don't set yourself—or your dog—up for failure.
- Be conscious of time, and plan ahead.
- Confine your dog prior to appointments, if she's prone to running away when called.

Jumping for Joy

ONE OF THE MOST ANNOYING BEHAVIORS PEOPLE experience is having their dogs jump on them and others when they walk through the door.

Dogs like to communicate with our faces because it is their social focal point. The closer they can get to our faces, the better! Why do you think dogs always lick your face and not your feet? No, it's not that Dr. Scholl's is a good friend, it's that your face is the most communicative part of your body.

As annoying as it is to be jumped on (well, by a dog anyway), don't resort to kneeing her in the chest or stepping on her toes, as some dog trainers would have you do! What are they thinking? Not only is it an insult to your dogs' expression of love, it can injure the dog, even breaking bones! Pain causes fear, fear causes low self-esteem, and low self-esteem causes behavior problems.

Never, *ever* stomp on your dog's toes or knee her in the chest. Would you do this to a child who wanted to sit in your lap? Not unless you were the Grinch! So, please don't do it to your dog. This kind of abusive behavior does *not* fall under my "whatever works" approach to dog training.

Your dog isn't trying to make you angry by jumping on you. She doesn't realize that she has mud on her feet or that her long toenails will rip your jacket. When she sees you, especially after a long separation, she's thinking, "There's the very best person on the planet, and I want to be closer to her." Her only thoughts are about how much she loves you; how she's waited all day to see you; and now, you're here!! She's not capable of assessing whether that's a real or faux silk blouse you're wearing, or whether your tie came from Italy or the secondhand store. Greeting her jumping like a demonically possessed football player will not create a bond—and it's a good way to make your dog fall out of love with you.

Dogs don't jump to make you mad or rip your clothing. They jump because they want to communicate with you by getting as close as they can to your face.

HELPFUL TECHNIQUES TO QUELL THE BOUNCIES

You can do several things to correct jumping behavior:

Dogs don't understand our system of manners, because it's okay for them to jump on other dogs in play.

1. Confine your dog to a designated space while you're gone, so that when you return, you have an opportunity to get through the door and can leash your dog before greeting her. Then, before you pet her, ask her to sit. Sitting automatically calms her and puts you in control over her behavior.

2. Actively ignore her. The moment she jumps, fold your arms and turn your back to her. This way, she can't engage your face, which is what she wants do. Don't look at her or speak to her until she stops jumping and settles down. Once settled, ask her to sit and then greet her. She will learn that she has to be in a sitting position before you will acknowledge her and give her attention. This technique quickly teaches your dog that it's no fun to jump, because she'll be ignored. However, it won't work on a dog that is willing to jump on your back when you turn away. Some dogs are just too excitable and will run their claws down

your back, causing a lot of pain. If these circumstances sound familiar, you might want to try technique 1 or 3.

3. Keep your dog on a street leash at all times, and control her when she jumps by pulling her toward the floor as you give the "off" command. A street leash, often called a "tab," is a short leash that clips to the collar and hangs about 12 to 16 inches (30.5–40.6 cm) below the dog's neck. The short leash prevents her from dragging a long one around all day and getting it caught on something. It is also more difficult to chew, because it doesn't extend beyond her chest area.

4. Use the shake can or squirt bottle. If possible, leave these items outside your door, so that you are fully equipped upon entry. As you administer the discipline with a squirt or shake, firmly say *"Off!"* Remember to praise her the second she stops jumping.

Bolting

SHE ROMPS THROUGH THE TALL, DANDELION- strangled grass, ears flopping like the wings of a happy dragonfly. She pants while running like a child rushing from one amusement park ride to another: "Come on! Come on! Hurry Mom, we might miss something!" She is your true companion, your protector . . . she is like your child—and now she is gone from your sight.

It's common for young dogs that lack exercise and discipline to challenge you to a "catch me if you can" game when you call them to you.

Even the most well-trained dog can be tempted to bolt when she sees another dog or animal in the distance. If your dog is especially social or predatory, it's bound to happen: one day, she'll run off, if she's not in your control.

Many people take their dogs out "unleashed," especially when good weather permits, to the beach or the park, and most never give a second thought to the risk this poses to the dog. It takes two seconds for your dog to bolt and put herself in danger, by running into the street or approaching an aggressive dog that she mistakes as friendly. Nor are all dogs directionally intelligent. Many have been picked up only blocks away from home, confused and lost. You could spend hours looking for a dog who has bolted, never knowing what kind of trouble she's getting into. Many dogs lose their way and never see their owners again.

A loose dog isn't always popular with others, either. Yours may be cordial at your holiday parties, but she won't necessarily be welcomed by strangers in a recreational area. Even dog lovers aren't thrilled with a roaming dog, and she may even run into one of those people who dislike dogs and find it fun to injure them.

Dogs bolt for the following reasons:

- **Lack of exercise**
- **Lack of socialization**
- **Hunger**
- **Sexual drive**
- **Abuse**
- **Fear of thunder or fireworks**
- **Chasing animals**
- **Chasing cars**
- **Chasing bicycles**
- **Chasing people**
- **Separation anxiety**
- **Searching for a deceased family member or dog**
- **Following a child to school or to the bus stop**

If your dog is prone to running off, consider getting her microchipped! Often, a lost dog will lose her collar in underbrush or when someone takes it off to see if the dog's name and phone number are written on the back. While the collar is being investigated, the dog runs off, never to be seen again. If

she is picked up by animal control, there is no way to know where she came from without a microchip.

Reconsider walking her off-leash. When she's in the yard, secure her with a tie-line or an unscalable fence. Dogs are capable of climbing fences 6 feet (1.8 m) high and higher, if their desire to escape confinement is great enough. If your dog bolts out the front door because your children are constantly coming in and out, or someone's always leaving the front door open, consider securing your dog in a part of the house that allows her to be part of daily activities but confined by a baby gate.

An invisible electric fence can work wonders for dogs that bolt. It can be a costly investment and requires some specific training to ensure that your dog is aware of her boundaries, but if you can afford it, it's probably the easiest approach to keeping your buddy safe and at home!

Out-of-Control Puppy Mouthing

AT FOUR TO FIVE MONTHS OF AGE, YOUR PUPPY IS teething and will feel the need to chew on something—you! Your skin is soft and warm, and you make fun, squeaky noises when she chomps down. When your puppy chews on you, don't wave your hands around, yell at her, or bop her on the nose. This kind of reaction stimulates her desire to play and will make her bite harder. When she was with her litter, it was natural and acceptable for her to play this way with her siblings. She doesn't understand that she can't behave like this with you. You're just as soft and warm . . . so, what's the difference?

The best way to change mouthing behavior is to simply replace the hand or body part being chewed with a chew toy. Make sure to praise her whenever she chews on something appropriate. To help ease her discomfort, which is partly the cause of the problem, cut some dish towels into strips, tie a few knots in each strip, saturate them with water, and put them in a freezer bag until they freeze solid. Offer your puppy a frozen strip to chew on daily. This helps to numb her gums and cut down on her desire to chew on everything in sight, including you.

Make sure she has plenty of chew toys with different textures to chew on throughout the day. Never offer her rawhide—it swells up to five times its original size in her belly and can take up to a week to digest. A puppy that eats rawhide every day can easily get an intestinal blockage, which is not only painful but requires surgery to fix. Stick to rubber and plastic chew toys made specifically for puppies. Many of these can be frozen and are just as enjoyable as a food chew.

If your puppy gets aggressively playful and expresses uncontrolled chewing or biting beyond the teething stage, you'll need to put her in The Big House for a time-out. I train puppies a bit differently than I train adult dogs, simply because puppies don't have the capacity to learn as quickly. Instead of enforcing the one-command-only technique I use for older dogs, I use "Three strikes, and you're out!" If, after firmly telling your puppy three times "No bite!" she still does not comply, put her in The Big House, a locked laundry room, or a bathroom for 5 or 10 minutes. You might find yourself putting her in time-out twenty times a day. That's okay! She'll quickly get the message that you mean business and that there is an unpleasant outcome with this behavior.

If you don't see results in a week, or feel that your puppy's behavior is abnormal, you'll need to call your vet for an examination. Your puppy might have medical issues.

Chapter Seven

Scaredy-Cats and Grumps

Dogs' emotions are very similar to ours. Just like humans, they get scared and become angry and frustrated—they even hurt people. When we hurt people, we know it's wrong. We're taught during childhood (well, many of us, anyway!) that it's wrong to hit, bite, and push others, and we grow up with laws to enforce this. Dogs just do what comes naturally. Although we expect them to understand our social standards and boundaries, it's equally important that we understand them, too!

As with people, however, a dog that's not taught proper behavior may end up being pushy, disliked by other dogs and people, or worse, become aggressive and anxious.

Leash Aggression

CAN YOU IMAGINE WHAT IT MUST BE LIKE TO TRY and establish a relationship while on a leash? It's hard enough just trying to elucidate your feelings through e-mail or find a good date! I can't imagine being chained to a six-foot leash and walked down the street every day through a crowd of my peers, with a super-tall being who doesn't speak my own language towering over me!

Many owners have problems with their dogs acting aggressively toward other dogs when they're on a leash. They don't know what to do, and many don't realize that it's a common problem. They feel embarrassed and unable to handle it. Often, a dog that acts aggressively on a leash exhibits no aggression when off-leash and will even be playful with other dogs. Talk about confusing!

Dogs become aggressive on a leash for several reasons: genetic predisposition, illness, territorial or owner protection, fear, and even a simple dislike of other dogs. Most of the time, a lack of exercise is the culprit. Ninety percent of pet dogs do not get the kind of physical release they need for their age, diet, and breed. Dogs need to run, and most of them need a minimum of 20 minutes of *aerobic* activity every day. Aerobic means any activity that uses large muscle groups, is rhythmic in nature, and is continuously maintained. It is the type of exercise that makes the heart and lungs work harder than when at rest. Running and playing hard with other dogs releases endorphins, the "feel-good" chemicals, which helps to create a happier and calmer dog. When your dog lacks endorphins, it can cause him, just like us, to be grumpy.

Taking your dog to an off-leash park can help him get the exercise he needs. Unfortunately, although they are on the rise, there are not enough *secure* off-leash dog parks accessible to every dog owner. Many people have social, playful dogs but can't enjoy the park because their dogs have a tendency to run off and the park lacks secure fencing around the perimeter. They're left feeling frustrated and stressed, and their dog ownership becomes a burden rather than something fun and rewarding.

Take the Dog by the Reins

Most adolescent dogs will, at some point, growl, bark, or lunge at another dog or person. The owner feels embarrassed and surprised and responds by tightening up on the leash, inadvertently escalating the situation because the dog is now responding to the signals from his owner. After several leash-aggression incidents, the dog owner may start to anticipate a situation while out on walks. As another dog approaches, the owner tightens up on the leash, so she can control the dog better. The dog, which has a keen sense of his master's body posture, begins to see what the owner is worried about—the other dog—and aggressive behavior ensues.

The first way to gain control over aggression is to teach your dog basic obedience (see chapter two, Basic Training). This will establish you as leader and give you more control over him. Then, during outings, relax your body posture and breathe deeply. Remind yourself that most dog scuffles never result in severe injury or drawn blood. As you relax, your body language will reflect this, and the more relaxed *you* are, the more relaxed your dog will be.

When you encounter an approaching dog, distract your dog by redirecting his attention before he has a chance to get out of control. Talk to him in a cheerful way, issuing a command that he knows and associates with pleasant things. If possible, change your direction to avoid a confrontation.

Learn to notice early warning signs. Note your dog's body language when he's calm and relaxed and how it changes when he becomes more aggressive. Look for changes around his head and neck—his hair standing up (hackles), eyes open wide—and if he is panting heavily and stiffening his gait.

At the first sign of a problem, ask your dog to sit. Sitting is a neutral, nonaggressive position. Use your hands to change his emotional state by stroking his head, mouth, or ears, and smoothing his hackles back into a more relaxed position. This is a rather uncommon technique, but it's very effective. Don't become consumed with petting, simply concentrate on changing your dog's body posture as you make him sit.

You should also control your own breathing and body posture by taking a deep breath and loosening any tension on the leash. When we get nervous, we tend to hold our breath and stiffen our gait. A dog can detect this tension in a heartbeat. Although you want to loosen your grip on the leash, avoid giving your dog complete freedom. Keep your hands positioned in such a way that you can quickly control him if an issue erupts.

It may seem scary when dogs growl and bark or snap at each other, but this behavior is little more than posturing and threats, designed to avoid real conflict. Remember, canine arguments rarely result in serious injury. Your dog uses his body language and vocalization in the same manner that we do, when we shout or yell at others in anger. Being aware of this fact should allow you to stay calmer and not imagine the worst!

Learn to distinguish between aggression and a response to rudeness. People often make the mistake of labeling a dog "aggressive," when he is simply defending himself from another dog's rudeness. This can happen when you're out for a stroll and another owner allows his dog to approach and engage in a rude, hostile, or inappropriate way by growling, sniffing aggressively, pawing, mounting, or even attacking. This behavior is no different than having a complete stranger come up and start kissing you! You wouldn't be considered an aggressive person if you snapped back or pushed him away. Far too many people allow their dogs to be rude to other dogs without realizing the kind of problems it creates. Dogs need to have manners, too!

Fear and Anger

WE HAVE BASICALLY FORCED DOGS TO BE HUMAN companions, but, although they seem to enjoy it, they will never be "human." We can't expect them to know how to behave and keep within appropriate boundaries when they are being assaulted by *us*. The attacker may only be a three-year-old running toward the dog like a drunk chimpanzee, but it's threatening, and a dog has a right to protect himself, doesn't he? Where are this child's parents? They are accountable for her behavior, yet it is the dog that gets blamed, sometimes even losing his life because of our irresponsibility.

A dog has no hands, so he uses his mouth for many functions. In addition to licking, playing with toys, eating, and barking, he uses it to communicate affection, submission, anxiety, and anger. I'm sure plenty of dogs would have chosen to slug someone, instead of biting them, but they can only use what they've got—teeth! Dog owners often don't understand their pets' emotions, reacting to their dog's behavior with anger and confusion. This just makes the problem worse, because the dog feels misunderstood.

If your dog has bitten a guest in an unprovoked manner, be sure to put the dog away when people come over. In the meantime, work on the issues with a behaviorist. If the behavior is severe—a child is brutally attacked, for example—the dog must go. However, if the child normally has a great relationship with the dog, and he nips her when she accidentally steps on his toes, you'll need to ask yourself if it's really necessary to re-home the dog. Often a dog is deemed aggressive if he only gives a warning, such as a snap or even just a growl, and he is then surrendered to the shelter, or even worse, euthanized. I find this so sad because things like this usually happen when there's a lack of supervision between the dog and child. If a two-year-old came up to me and pulled my eyelashes, I might snap at her, too!

I'm not advocating that anybody keep an aggressive dog, especially if he or she has children. As a responsible parent, you need to keep your children safe. However, there are levels of aggressive dog behavior, and many can be changed if people put themselves in the dog's position, for just one moment, and educate themselves about the causes of aggression.

Fear Aggression

MANY DOGS HAVE FEAR AND ANXIETY ISSUES.
Although he may not remember what he did 60 seconds ago, he clearly remembers people who have injured or abused him. Shelter dogs have at least one unpleasant memory from their past, if not a trunk full! Just as we have fears and bad dreams after watching scary movies or enduring a frightening or traumatizing event, so does your dog.

Dogs often exhibit aggression toward strangers who resemble people that have hurt them in the past. This is *fear aggression*. A person on the street wearing a red hat, for example, triggers your dog's memory of an abusive owner who always wore a red baseball hat. Fearful that the abusive person

has returned and is attempting to take him away from his now loving and non-abusive parent, he may react by lashing out and attempting to bite the person. You're left shocked and confused at his behavior, wondering if your dog has a mental problem!

For serious cases—if your dog has bitten or attempted to bite someone, for example—it's important to work with an animal behaviorist who can create a personalized behavior modification plan. If that alone doesn't work, consider getting some short-term (three months) psychoactive medication from your veterinarian. It can help calm your dog's disposition and often has a lasting

effect, even after the medication has been discontinued. However, you will want to continue with behavior modification until your dog appears stable and fear-free.

The Body Language of Fear

- **Tail tucked under bottom**
- **Ears back flat against head**
- **Head lowered with cowering-type behavior**
- **Frequent licking of lips**
- **Nervous behavior and frequent yawning**
- **Body shivering**

Puppies that are exceptionally fearful of the world around them generally stay that way when they grow up.

Dogs enjoy small, dark spaces, such as crates and under blankets, when feeling nervous.

When your dog is stressed or anxious, make sure he has a dark, safe place to retreat to: a crate, a closet, or under a bed or blanket, for example. Events such as holiday parties and family gatherings can be very stressful for your dog, especially if little children are present. Young children can be physically rough with pets, and older ones are prone to teasing them. Teach your guests, especially children, not to approach the dog when he is in his special space. A dog that loves children and is otherwise friendly can bite anyone who pushes his boundaries when he is scared.

Dominance and Territorial Aggression

THREE OF THE MOST COMMON types of aggression are *dominance aggression, territorial aggression*, and fear aggression (described on page 140). Aggression does not always result in an injury, but it is usually preceded by warnings signs, such as growling, snapping, nipping, and/or running away.

A dominant dog may bite if he does not like a child picking up one of his toys, getting near his food or bone, or pulling on his ears or tail. This is dominance aggression.

A territorial dog may bite an uninvited stranger who enters his property or walks through the door, even if he or she is welcomed by the dog's owners. This is territorial aggression. A dog exhibiting this behavior is signifying to his owner that he or she is not really the leader of the pack. Instead of looking to the human for reassurance that the situation is acceptable, the dog with territorial aggression instinctively dislikes the stranger and attempts to control the situation with scare tactics. A person who is Alpha in the dog's eyes has basically said, "This is my home, and if I say this person can enter, he can, so back off."

Aggression can be caused by

- **Genetic predisposition**
- **Allergic reaction to chemicals in food**
- **Lack of proper behavior training**
- **Type of breed**
- **Being a dominant dog lacking leadership from "human" family pack**
- **Lack of socialization with other dogs during adolescence**
- **Imprinting by an aggressive or fearful mother or father that "people are bad"**

- **Living in the wild for a period of time and having to fend for oneself**
- **Emotional trauma due to abuse or injury**
- **Being attacked repeatedly by other dogs in family pack or at a dog park**
- **Thyroid malfunction or other medical conditions, such as brain tumor**
- **Lack of proper nutrition and care**
- **Neglect and starvation**

If aggressive or fearful behavior arises out of nowhere in your otherwise friendly dog, it could mean that he is ill or has an undiscovered injury. If he becomes aggressive with someone, never make the mistake of becoming aggressive in return. The best reaction is a firm command of "No!" Whether your dog has bitten or just threatened someone, the first thing to do is lead your dog to a secure, quiet place before attempting to address the victim. Once the situation is handled, schedule a medical visit with your vet, so he or she can examine your dog and help uncover whether the reasons behind the acute change of behavior are emotional or physical. Your vet will most likely advise you to seek immediate assistance from a professional in the field of canine aggression.

Meanwhile, keep your dog away from the public, especially children. If your dog has indeed bitten someone, it's possible, especially if your dog's rabies vaccination is not up to date, that animal control may remove him from the home and put him into quarantine for 10 days. He may even be destroyed, depending on his breed and aggressive history and the severity of the incident. When a dog bites once, it's easier for him to bite again if he knows he can get away with it. The biggest factor in your overall success of getting a handle on your grumpy pup is to prevent him from biting at the first sign of aggression.

Many dog bites occur when a dog is being territorial by protecting his home.

- Growling—showing teeth or closed-mouthed
- Guarding—food bowl, treats, toys, possessions, resting spot, person, or other pet. This is a highly volatile and dangerous situation, in which children are in immediate danger. The dog will not always growl, but he may have a strange, wide-eyed look on his face and will often glance sideways.
- Snap and miss—dogs have amazing distance perception, and when they miss, it's on purpose. It's a warning that a bite is imminent.
- Snarl—a sort of snort and growl that might even contain a small bark
- Aggressive barking —out of control barking in which teeth are being shown
- Hackles up—hair standing up on neck and back
- Lunging on or off the leash— showing teeth, growling, or barking
- Raising the tail—when people approach; may not apply to breeds with naturally curled tails, such as Chihuahua, pug, husky, and Akita

Keeping Safe

Never approach an unfamiliar dog—especially an unfamiliar dog that is ill, sleeping, eating, chewing on a toy, or caring for puppies.

Never pet an unfamiliar dog by reaching over his head. People forget their size relative to dogs, and many dogs, even secure and friendly ones, are scared by strangers looming over and reaching toward them. Always offer your hand first, to allow the dog to sniff you and invite you to pet him, then reach under his chin and pet the side of his face, under his chin, or on his chest.

Never stare a dog directly in the eye; he will consider this a challenge. Keep sight of him to protect yourself, but avert your gaze.

If an aggressive-looking dog is stalking you, never scream and run; this only triggers his predatory drive, and he will chase—and catch—you. Grab a stick or a rock to defend yourself should an attack ensue. As long as he is not attacking you, remain motionless. If he doesn't find you a threat, he may leave you alone. Shout, "Off!" or "No!" in a deep voice, and growl at the dog as if you are not afraid. This may make him think twice about attacking you. Dogs have instincts that make them stop and think: "I might get hurt. Is this worth it?"

If you're wearing a sweater or a jacket, take it off and wrap it around your forearm, as slowly as you can, so as not to trigger the attack sooner. Offer that arm to him if he insists on attacking you. When attacking, most dogs will bite the body part closest to the mouth; this is usually a leg, because people tend to kick at the dog in self-defense.

If you're knocked over by the dog prior to attack, roll into a ball, lock your fingers together behind your neck, and bring your elbows down over your ears and neck to protect your main artery from being punctured. You can withstand many bites, but a punctured jugular vein can prove fatal.

If you have a small dog with you, picking him up to protect him will make it tricky to roll into a ball. If the attacking dog knocks you down with your pooch in your arms, get on your hands and elbows, allowing some space underneath your body to protect your dog, and cover your neck and head as much as possible. If you have a medium-to-large dog with you, chances are, he can protect himself against the offender better than you can. Let him loose, so he doesn't entangle himself or you in the leash.

Finally, scream *"Help!"* repeatedly. Most people will take that seriously and investigate or call 911.

Child Safety

Never allow an unattended baby or a young child to be around your dog, or any-one else's, if he is aggressive, territorial, or dominant. Children innocently pull on ears and tails, pick up dog toys, and approach eating and sleeping dogs with-out caution. Most attacks on children are committed by dogs that are otherwise gentle and nonaggressive. However, when they are eating, sleeping, or in pain, they can lash out and, within seconds, cause permanent and sometimes fatal injuries. A jealous, dominant dog may wait until he is alone with the child to show her that he's the pack leader. His attempt to scare the child can result in major injury or death.

CHILD SAFETY TIPS

- Never leave children unsupervised around dogs.

- Teach your children to ask a dog owner if it's okay to pet the dog.

- Teach your children to pet a dog under its chin and not by reaching over his back or head.

- When children are young, guide their hands, showing them where to pet the dog, so they learn to touch him gently.

- Teach them never to run at a dog or pull its tail or ears.

- Remind them that animals hurt, too, and to be careful when they are playing near the dog.

If properly taught by a parent, a child as young as eight can establish a respect-based relationship with his dog. Still, because there is so much room for error when children are involved, a parent must always be present. At some point, every dog, regardless of breed or age, will try to challenge its owner. This is normal for dogs, and occurs during canine adolescence, between 7 and 14 months of age.

Bringing Home A Baby

Bringing home a new baby means having less time for your dog than you did before. Make the changes to the dog's routine slowly, before the baby is born. Have the dog spend some time around children (supervised, of course), so he gets used to them and you can see if he appears to like them. Most people know the spots on their dog's body that might be sensitive to pinching from little fingers. Practice handling your dog in the way a child might, such as gently pulling on ears, tail, or paws, and reward the dog if he sits nicely without a negative reaction. You might also teach him how to gently accept food from a hand.

You can help your dog acclimate to his new human sibling by bringing home a blanket with the baby's smell on it prior to the baby's homecoming. To prevent feelings of anger and resentment toward the new baby, show your dog twice as much attention and offer special treats to him when the baby is around. This helps create a positive association with the baby. Taking your dog on special outings that do not involve the baby, but are only about the dog having fun, helps to keep that dog-human bond and quells Fido's possible feelings of rejection.

Until you can gauge your dog's temperament toward the new baby, make sure that your dog is leashed and held by Dad during the greeting process. This helps control him without too much fuss, if he acts strangely and wants to get too close a look. I also suggest placing a baby gate at the entrance of the nursery, to prevent the dog from visiting the baby unattended.

If you notice that your dog seems uninterested or even upset about the baby, don't fret. It can take some time for your dog to bond with this new pup and accept her into the pack. Keep giving him plenty of attention and special one-on-one time with you, and he'll be ready to play big brother in no time flat!

Separation Anxiety

DOGS REACT TO STRESS AND CHANGE, just like we do. However, because they can't express themselves verbally, they express anxiety through potty issues, destructive behavior, and sometimes even self-induced injury. Your dog may become anxious and depressed for several reasons, many of which can be related to changes in your life: moving to a new home, a family member leaving for college, a divorce or separation, a new baby, domestic issues between you and your spouse, a death, an illness, or even just a change in your dog's normal daily routine.

Seasonal changes can also have an effect, preventing you from enjoying the outdoors with your dog, the way you did during warmer weather. Dogs need to get out and exercise every day to release their pent-up energy. Playing ball on the living room floor won't cut it. Without proper exercise, dogs can become depressed, and that depression turns into anxiety—especially when they're left alone.

The cause of separation anxiety is that your dog thinks you're *never coming back* and he's going to be confined in this space forever. This causes panic, which in turn causes the dog to relieve his stress by chewing, digging, howling, barking, or attempting to escape. Dogs don't view time the way we do. If your dog was once abandoned or neglected by another owner, this problem will be ten times worse!

Many people compound the problem, trying to eliminate the destruction by locking their anxious dog in a crate. This creates confinement panic and makes the dog feel even more trapped and desperate to escape. A dog can break teeth, nails, and sometimes even toes trying to escape the crate. There have also been reports of dogs jumping through plate glass windows in a panic to find their owners.

A common problem anxious dogs develop is a self-calming but mutilating obsessive-compulsive disorder called *acral lick granuloma*. A dog with this disorder relieves stress by repeatedly licking and chewing at a certain spot on his leg or hind quarters until he has created an ulcer-like sore. In most cases, treating the skin lesion is not enough, as many dogs will just find a new spot on which to chew. Just giving the dog more attention and playtime can sometimes alleviate this problem.

Symptoms of Separation Anxiety

- **Whining**
- **Pacing**
- **Panting**
- **Excessive drooling**
- **Defecating**
- **Urinating**
- **Barking and yelping**
- **Howling and crying**
- **Dilated pupils**
- **Depression**

- **Overeating**
- **Anxiety anorexia (refusing to eat or drink in owner's absence)**
- **Destruction of house and personal objects**
- **Ingestion of nonfood items, such as plastics and paper**
- **Self-mutilation (chewing on or licking body)**
- **Frequent solicitation of attention and affection**
- **Excessive greetings at door**

You can help your dog feel more comfortable in your absence in a number of ways. One approach is to leave for short periods of time, several times a day. Take the car around the block a few times (that is, if your neighbors won't think you've lost your mind!). Short durations of absence help your dog learn that leaving doesn't always mean forever. Remember to praise your dog and give him a treat if he is sitting quietly and calmly when you walk back in. If he's being overly hyper and attentive, say hello, smile, and walk away from him. Doting on him when he's emotional reinforces his distress, in much the way a mother's overreaction causes a child to cry when he falls down. By keeping your return casual and calm, his response won't be conditioned in a negative way.

Once your dog finally settles, give him lots of love. Play with a ball or offer to take him for a walk. This helps reinforce that being calm when you're gone, and when you come home, results in good things.

Other ways to alleviate separation anxiety:

- **If possible, hide departure triggers, such as familiar coats, jackets, purses, briefcases, and keys, by keeping them in the garage, the car, a duffle bag, or another location away from the front door.**

- **If you can, vary the times of day you leave and the duration of your absence.**

- Muffle your keychain in a sock or glove, and place it in your pocket or purse. Use a single (quiet) key on a string of yarn to lock and unlock the door upon departure and arrival.

- Leave the TV or radio on while you're gone, to reduce outdoor noises that may trigger anxiety.

- Exercise your dog daily, especially with aerobic activity, such as hard running, for at least 20 minutes. Be careful not to run him too hard in hot weather, and choose breed-specific exercise, to avoid injuring your dog. Check with your vet before you begin any new physical regimen for your dog.

- Enroll your dog in a doggy day care program, so he can play daily with other dogs and enjoy the socialization he needs. If your dog is not "dog-friendly," hire a teenager or professional dog walker to take him for daily walks and runs.

- If you must leave your dog at home, give him something to chew on to keep him occupied.

- Give your dog a crate to hide in during the day, filling it with treats, toys, and an article of clothing with your scent on it. If he appears to like his new den, but still has destructive or potty issues while you're gone, consider confining him in the crate by actually closing the door. Although most dogs are completely fine with this, shelter dogs often have confinement issues. Be sure to hang around, out of sight, the first couple of times you try this out, to make sure your dog does not panic.

If all else fails, talk to your vet about short-term medication, which can help quell the anxiety and change your dog's behavior. Antianxiety medications can permanently cure the problem by changing the receptors in your dog's brain. If your dog has injured himself, call your vet right away. Reducing the risk of injury to your dog has priority over gaining control of this issue.

CRATE CONFINEMENT RULES OF THUMB

Age in months equals hours in the crate. In other words, two months equals two hours; three months equals three hours; four months equals four hours; and so on, until your dog reaches nine or ten months of age, and then you can expect an all day or night hold. If you can't accommodate these crate times, I suggest putting your dog in a confined space with a baby gate.

Case Study

LUCKY'S STORY

Dave was a bachelor who lived on five acres. He was in charge of his own schedule when he adopted a toy fox terrier named Lucky. Fox terriers are a high-energy breed that need a lot of exercise and entertainment, which Dave was able to provide, by taking Lucky on hikes into the hills and bike rides through the forest trails. A couple of years later, however, Dave landed a full-time job in the city. He sold his land and bought a condo. Lucky no longer had forest trails and acres of land to run on. In fact, he now didn't even have a backyard.

Dave was gone from 8:00 AM to 5:00 PM, Monday through Friday, and was so tired by the end of the day that he didn't have the energy to take Lucky for a walk, except on the weekends. He threw the ball across the living room occasionally, which took up some of Lucky's energy, but it wasn't the same. Lucky slowly grew bored, overweight, and anxious.

Dave came home one night to find a note on his door about Lucky whining and howling while he was gone. The next day he left the radio on, thinking it would help Lucky feel less alone, but Lucky just howled more loudly—which became a real problem for the neighbors. Feeling helpless, and worried about getting kicked out of his apartment, Dave bought Lucky a bark collar. The collar sprayed a fine mist of citronella oil in front of Lucky's nose whenever he barked or howled.

Lucky quickly learned to stop barking and howling. However, he had to release his anxiety in some way, so he started ripping up a woven living room rug. Dave came home to find Lucky's leg entangled in the threads of the rug. The leg was swollen and bleeding, because he had struggled for hours to get free. Poor Lucky lay on the floor completely exhausted. Dave was beside himself, knowing he had to do something, but what? After speaking with friends, he was referred to me.

I knew right away that Lucky was suffering from separation anxiety, so I asked Dave if it was possible for him to move to a place with a backyard or take Lucky to work with him for a few hours a day. Dave said no. This meant Lucky needed a way to handle being at home without letting his separation anxiety get the better of him. I suggested that Dave send Lucky to doggy day care. This would provide an outlet for his energy reserve, help to create the flow of endorphins to the brain, and keep Lucky happy and socialized in Dave's absence. He followed my advice but couldn't afford to place Lucky in day care every day of the week.

I advised Dave to get a plastic crate for Lucky to use when on the days when he was at home. Dave covered it on three sides with a dark blanket and filled it with new toys and treats, so that Lucky would have a safe and entertaining place to "den" when he was anxious. I also told him to secure the door open with a tieback, to prevent it from accidentally closing while Lucky was in it, scaring him and discouraging him from using the crate again. Not only did it work, but at night, Lucky slept in the crate, instead of in his dog bed, which exposed him in all directions.

Although Lucky loved to run and play, he needed a safe haven during his times alone. I also suggested that Dave leave in the crate a T-shirt with his scent on it, along with a pet-safe stuffed animal for Lucky to cuddle with. This, combined with leaving a radio or the TV on during the day, also helped Lucky feel more secure.

Dave told me that Lucky started getting anxious about thirty minutes before he left every day. To help him gain long-term success, I suggested that he alter his morning routine. Because Lucky's anxiety was triggered by seeing Dave put his jacket on and hearing the rattling of the car keys, I told Dave to leave his keys, and even his jacket, in the car at night (he had an indoor garage). In this way, he eliminated the cues that made Lucky so upset. I also encouraged Dave to get a treat toy from the pet store and fill the holes with all-natural peanut butter or cheese, giving it to Lucky before leaving to distract him and form a positive association with Dave's departure (*see* chapter one). Dave gave it to him *only* before he left the house and at no other time, to help Lucky form a positive, happy feeling about saying goodbye.

Lastly, I suggested that Dave buy some Bach Flower Remedy and administer it orally, four drops at a time, in the morning and evening. (Bach Flower Remedy doesn't always work, however, and sometimes a more conventional medical intervention is necessary.) Dave followed my advice, administering Bach Flower Remedy daily and hiring a teenager to come in every day after school to play with and walk Lucky when he couldn't visit day care. Lucky is now anxiety-free, and, three years later, both he and Dave are doing just great!

Chapter Eight

You Silly Dog!

Dogs can have silly habits—barking at shadows, chasing their tails, snapping at flies—that we often find amusing. Reinforced by human attention, such as laughter or even a command to produce the habit for entertainment purposes, the behavior is repeated over and over until the once-adorable habit is just annoying— and the dog is on her way to developing severe behavioral issues. The action that once garnered a pleasant response and made her feel like a star is now met with a reprimand, making her feel like a fool—and making life difficult for you.

- Don't give your dog attention when she's chasing her tail.
- Get up, ring a bell, and walk out of the room.
- Only engage her when she stops the behavior, then praise her for it.
- Exercise her more frequently.
- Limit her sugar and chemical intake, as discussed in chapter one.

Chasing Cars

CANINE CAR CHASERS ARE A MENACE, NOT ONLY TO THEMSELVES BUT TO drivers. Most breeds prone to this behavior are in the herding and hunting category. Some perceive moving vehicles as motorized stray sheep and attempt to herd them back to the flock. Other dogs may be expressing their territorial rights by literally driving away the intruder from what they consider their street, or 'hood. It's a very rewarding sport, you see, because the dog is always successful—she chases the car, it goes away. I wish I could do that with cellulite.

Dogs that have been thrown from a car or abandoned on the highway see cars as something to be hated. Dogs that have been hit by cars see them as something to be feared. In both cases, the dog reacts to the car out of self-defense, thinking that by chasing it away, the bad thing won't happen to her again. For example, a re-homed and happy dog that was abused by someone with a blue truck will react aggressively when she sees a blue truck, sometimes even biting at tires, moving or not. Fearing that the abusive person is back to reclaim her, she attempts to chase the person/truck away. Sadly, this behavior too often results in the demise of the dog.

Consider your dog's history and try to determine why she chases cars. If you think it might be due to some past trauma, check with your vet. X-rays may reveal previously broken bones and provide a clue to her past. If your dog is a herding breed that chases everything in sight, she's likely chasing cars out of a predatory drive or because she's bored. The most common-sense approach to deterring car-chasing behavior is to keep your dog from being off-leash outside. But this is the real world, and this is not always possible.

If your dog only chases a particular vehicle, such as a postal van that visits the neighborhood on a regular basis, she might just need a nice introduction. Have the offending van driver offer her a treat from inside the vehicle. Once she sees that this vehicle and its person are a giving tree, not an intruder, the problem will be solved. The more positive associations your dog can make with any kind of vehicle, the less threatened she'll be.

Regardless of your dog's reason for chasing cars, even if it's due to emotional trauma, she's usually suffering from a lack of exercise and social stimuli. If it's not possible to arrange play dates or take your dog to the dog park because she's not a social dog, find other ways to offer aerobic activity, such as taking agility classes, learning dog tricks, or even herding sheep! Aerobic exercise increases the happy chemicals in her brain and helps blow off some major steam.

Chasing the Tail

TAIL CHASING CAN BECOME A REALLY ANNOYING habit, after a while—and you might be responsible for it. Why? Generally when a dog finds her tail and becomes enamored with it, you think it's funny. Watching your cute little fuzzball whirl like a dervish makes you laugh, so you encourage her to continue or repeat it. Once she learns that this behavior attracts attention, she starts doing it every time she wants attention from you. Now, you can't make her stop.

What follows is that she will start to exhibit this behavior as a response to boredom and/or stress. It becomes an autonomic response, functionally independent of rational thought, causing her to spin out of control. The minute you get upset, yell at her, or ignore her, she becomes stressed, exacerbating the behavior. Telling her to stop just perpetuates the problem, because you're still giving her the atten-tion she seeks. Even though she only gets negative attention by behaving this way, it's just fine with her, as long as she's getting *some* kind of attention.

To break the cycle, ring a bell. This breaks the connection between the brain and the tail. The sound of the bell will alert her to the fact that you're getting up and walking out of the room. Now, no one is left to perform for, and no performer likes an empty room.

Ignore her completely until she follows you. Then smile and give her positive attention. If she follows you and starts chasing her tail again, ring the bell and walk away to another room. Be persistent. Even if you have to do this twenty times a day, do not look at or talk to her until she stops. The minute she does, praise her calmly, so she doesn't get excited again. If she doesn't seem to improve, consult your vet about giving her some short-term anti-anxiety medication.

Chasing Shadows and Lights

CHASING SHADOWS AND LIGHTS ISN'T A COMMON problem with dogs. For some, it's not a problem at all; it's just a way to combat boredom.

Dogs who exhibit this behavior are generally high-strung, predatory in nature, and under-exercised. A dog lacking social stimulus can project her desire for a playmate by practicing this behavior in an obsessive-compulsive way. Although she learned in puppyhood what her shadow was, her lack of social life causes her to see the shadows as imaginary playmates. To quell this desire, enroll her in doggy day care, hire a dog walker, or arrange playdates with other playful dogs.

Laser pointers, originally intended to provide cats with stimulation, can provide entertainment for dogs, because they instigate a prey response. Most dogs like to chase "something," and because they can't hurt a laser light people think it's a great way to exercise the dog. The idea is great, but once Fido starts, he just can't seem to stop. Many dogs won't stop searching for the light, and it becomes a compulsive behavior.

If your dog has become addicted to moving lights, replace this stimulus with something like a ball on a string, which she can chase and ultimately conquer. The satisfaction that comes from frequent victory will eventually outweigh the excitement of pursuing lights and shadows.

Sometimes, no matter what you do, a dog can take light and shadow chasing to such extremes that she becomes completely consumed by it, and it can be hard to distract her from the behavior. She may even stop sleeping, eating, or drinking. At this point, you may want to seek medical intervention, but until then, giving her plenty of exercise can help to reduce the frequency and duration of this behavior.

If the problem becomes so serious that your dog is actually biting the wall to get at shadows and lights, causing damage to her teeth and your home, you might have to confine her. You might also need to see your vet about medications for this excessively compulsive behavior.

Chasing Other Animals

Canines aren't the only ones with a predatory drive. Humans have one, as well. Consider the way children chase each other. Although the intent is not to catch and eat one another, we wouldn't behave this way in play if we weren't somehow predatorily hardwired, too. Along with domestic dogs, we evolved over time into creatures who have our prey delivered to us (unless we are hunters). Predatory skills form the foundation for human survival—they have made it possible for dogs and humans to coexist and form a remarkable relationship.

Dogs chase other animals because it's fun and it satiates their primal need. It doesn't mean that your dog will harm the cat if she catches it, but someone will get a poke in the eye, for sure! However, certain breeds are very predatory in nature and sometimes enjoy a little snack, so never encourage your dog to chase any animal, even a bird or squirrel. It can come back to haunt you when Fido goes after your neighbor's cat and succeeds in catching it. Although you will rarely be able to effectively remove your dog's inherent instincts, you can alleviate chasing behavior by giving your dog more exercise, using a leash on walks, and verbally disciplining the behavior when it occurs.

Signs of Predatory Behavior:

- **Running back and forth, with nose to ground**
- **Sniffing the air, perhaps running from side to side**
- **Head raised, ears erect, eyes wide**
- **Running forward, then stopping abruptly to listen**
- **Whining and panting**
- **Drooling**
- **Barking**
- **Marking**
- **Pulling on leash**

ANCESTORS OF DOMESTIC DOGS were carnivorous, predatory creatures. They had to be to survive. Our dogs are still hardwired, to some extent, with a predatory drive. Reversion to predatory behavior is not only normal but, for some dogs—working or herding breeds, for example—absolutely necessary for mental well-being.

Excessive Licking

Dogs that lick themselves repeatedly may be suffering from anxiety or allergies.

DOGS LICK TO CLEAN THEMSELVES, STIMULATE their young to eliminate, taste a particular scent, show submission, and comfort a wound. However, allergies, bug bites, or dry skin can cause a dog to lick excessively at a "hot spot," also called an *acral lick granuloma,* an area of the dog's skin that has become itchy and inflamed. The excessive daily licking soon causes a skin sore or ulcer to appear that, when chewed and licked to relieve the pain and itching, often aggravates the wound and inhibits healing. Anti-itch medications, skin ointments, and hyposensitizing allergy shots can ease symptoms, but medical intervention to keep the dog from licking the wound (such as a halo collar—a plastic, funnel-like collar that attaches to the dog's neck and prevents him from turning backwards to lick) is usually needed to heal the wound properly. If a bacterial infection is suspected, antibiotics must be used for at least six to eight weeks.

Injuries such as bone infections, bacterial skin infections, parasites, and other physical problems can also cause acral lick granulomas to occur. One of the best medications for allergic-type lick granuloma is hydrocortisone, which you can get from your vet.

Some skin ulcers are thought to be brought on by stress or boredom, and can be related to obsessive-compulsive disorders. Dogs suffering from psychological licking can respond to simple changes in their environment. Increase the activity and human attention your dog receives to reduce stress, anxiety, and boredom.

Dogs are sensitive and need attention and affection, just like we do. If your dog is affectionate and really enjoys human interaction, making him live outside or in dirty living conditions and providing poor nutrition could lead to excessive licking issues. For some cases, a vet may prescribe a short-term low dose of anti-anxiety or antidepressant medication, such as Elavil, Trexane, Anafranil, or Prozac. Acupuncture can also be highly effective for some dogs, but it may not always be available in your locale.

For whatever reason your dog is licking, if it appears excessive, tell her "No," and without rewarding her behavior, try to distract her from it. Often, a bath with colloidal oatmeal and olive oil can help to soothe irritated skin (yours, too!), until you can make an appointment with the vet.

Licking Genitals and Feet

Excessive licking of the genitals and feet is usually caused by yeast problems, created by too much sugar in the diet (see chapter one) or certain medications. Yeast bacteria, which create an itchy rash, thrive and multiply in warm, moist places of the body, such as in folds of the upper inside leg and between the toes, sometimes even in the ears. The much-wrinkled shar-pei breed often has trouble with yeast rashes in the loose folds of its face and body. Great care must be taken in warm climates to assure the cleanliness of this breed.

Excessive licking of the genitals can also be a symptom of impacted anal sacs. Anal sacs become impacted when they fail to empty with bowel movements, as they normally do. Too many soft stools or an overactive gland may cause the anal secretions to become too thick to be eliminated naturally. If your dog's anal area is itchy and impacted, you may notice her scooting her behind along the floor or rubbing her rear end against furniture. Many dogs never need to have their anal sacs expressed, but some require frequent trips to the vet.

Groomers generally provide this service during the bathing process. If you notice symptoms of impacted anal sacs emerging, ask your groomer to express them, then ask your vet to help you uncover the reasons for the problem.

Dogs mainly lick people to show respect.

Licking People

Most licking by your dog is shown as a sign of respect or deference. Puppies in the wild often show this behavior to express respect or hunger when the Alpha comes back to the den from an absence. A nondominant adult dog exhibiting this behavior usually lowers her head and body to make herself smaller, almost mimicking juvenile behavior. The Alpha receiving the face licks expresses dominance by standing tall to accept the respectful gesture but does not reciprocate.

Shelter dogs and dogs that are submissive by nature often lick for acceptance from their human caregivers. Dogs with low self-esteem needing constant reassurance and acceptance will lick your legs, feet, and face excessively.

Dominant dogs, usually males, sometimes lick the face of a person they consider their mate or force their licking, in an annoying and negative way, on someone they view as beneath them in the hierarchy. Dominant licking should never be tolerated, especially toward children. The minute you suspect that your dog is licking in a dominant way, say "No lick!" Then, remove him from the target person and make him sit. If you are consistent with this approach, you'll be able to *lick* this licking, in no time flat!

Reasons for licking:

- **A dam, or mother dog, licks her newborn pups to awaken them from their postpartum sleepiness, to stimulate them to eliminate, and to bond with and comfort them.**

- **Pups lick their dam's lips when they want food.**

- **Licking by pups, as well as adult dogs, is a sign of submission and respect.**

PAWSITIVELY SOOTHING TUSCAN BATH CRÈME

1 tsp (5 ml) European sea salt

1/2 cup (120 ml) extra virgin olive oil

1/2 cup (120 ml) colloidal oatmeal

1 cup (235 ml) baby shampoo

2 tsp (10 ml) tea tree oil

1 ounce (28 g) dried, crushed lavender

Mix ingredients together. Wet your dog and pour the bath crème onto her fur. Lather the body and wound with bath crème, leaving it on for 1 minute. Rinse with warm water.

Humping

Most humping behavior, which can be very embarrassing for the dog owner, is really only about dominance and play, and is not generally sexual in nature.

BEHAVIOR PROBLEMS CAN START FOR PHYSICAL reasons and then continue because they have become habits. Humping is a prime example. Most of the humping that your puppy does is simply play. But if the behavior persists into adulthood, it's often because he derived some kind of pleasure from it and was able to practice it for prolonged periods with another dog or an object. If you're not blushing too much yet, let's move on.

Dogs Humping Dogs

Juvenile dogs often hump (or attempt to hump) other dogs to test their boundaries. Because they are dominant, immature, and exploring the social world around them, they end up taking a few knocks from other dogs before they understand what's acceptable and what's not, as far as social behavior is concerned.

A dog's size is not a significant dominance factor in family packs. A small dog that is the Alpha of his pack will hump the leg of a bigger dog, to keep him in line. A smaller dog might also rudely goose the bigger dog's rear with his nose—just to show him that size doesn't matter.

If your dog persists in humping other, unknown, dogs in an unwelcome manner, it's probably best to separate your dog from his victim. Although it's often just an annoyance to the other dog, if he is dominant, the perceived assault can result in your dog being seriously injured.

Consistently keeping control over how much humping your dog does prevents it from becoming an obsessive habit. With that said, if your dog is playing well with another dog and testing out his humping dominance in a playful way, I wouldn't worry too much about it, especially if the other dog doesn't seem to mind or responds with the same behavior.

Humping can become a problem when a female dog is in heat, and many males in the vicinity will try to become frisky with her. Jealousy among her suitors can cause a fight to break out and could result in unwanted pregnancy. During this time, it's best to keep your hot momma behind closed doors!

Neutering a male dog, especially if he's dominant, can help with humping issues, but it is not always a guaranteed cure, and it can take many months before hormone levels decrease enough to show a change in desire. To gain the upper hand on this behavior, put your dog through some obedience courses, so you have more control over him when he's in the presence of other dogs. You may also want to work on the dominance-related techniques found in chapters one and two.

Dogs Humping People

Humping is a natural dog-to-dog behavior, but when your new slacks are at risk from "Henry the Humping Hound," you need to draw the line! Dogs hump people for reasons that vary from simply liking a person or being overexcited to expressing dominance over them. I've even witnessed a dog "hump air" for prolonged periods when he became overly excited at his master's arrival. It was really quite a funny sight! However, laughing and encouraging the dog to perform in this manner only makes the problem worse. His owner has no control over his humping-of-the-air habit, nor where or when it will happen. "Nice to meet you, your highness! This is my dog *Hump*hrey."

Big dominant dogs often attempt to hump children and small adults because they have a strength and height advantage. Little dominant dogs may attempt to hump adults but will most likely have a go at small children and/or objects such as pillows. An insecure "only dog" might hump inanimate objects when at home, as way to relieve stress-related insecurity issues caused by the prior presence of other dogs, especially if he's been beaten up once or twice. By expressing this behavior, he's showing his dominance over something he knows can't react aggressively, thereby making him feel more self-confident. This behavior is similar to the relief we feel when we unleash on a punching bag. A better way to help him build his self-confidence is to enroll him in dog agility classes. If he's a working breed, he can even learn to let off steam at a facility that teaches dogs to herd sheep!

Don't let your dog hump your children or their friends. Talk to your children, and make sure that they and their friends don't try to trigger this behavior because they think it's funny. They need to know that this behavior is a problem for you, that it embarrasses you, and that you expect them to respect your wishes.

The most helpful way to change your dog's behavior is through simple obedience training. If your dog attempts to hump someone, tell him "No! Sit!" Ask the person he was trying to hump to say "No!" as well and to ignore him completely. This way, the dog will understand that it's not just you, but also the object of his affection, canceling this provocative pursuit. If he persists, create a negative association to the behavior by removing him to a crate or into the backyard or the laundry room, isolating him until your guest leaves. The more he receives this response, the less likely he'll be to act up, if he wants to hang around.

Dogs will try to hump humans to show dominance over them.

Conclusion

DOGS STRIVE AS HARD TO UNDERSTAND US as we do to understand them. The one thing dogs particularly want you to understand is that they are not trying to be a problem. They are trying to love you in the best way they know. Sometimes love hurts, but we can't live without it, just as we can't live without these furry little angels that bestow so much magic to our everyday, sometimes boring, lives. Life just wouldn't be the same without them. Consider how bland our daily existence would be without needing to clean bits of dog food from between our toes, without loitering for what seems like hours in the cleaning aisle at the supermarket, searching for that perfect spray to remove dried-on drool from your antique settee. What would you do without that mysterious odor, wafting up, ever so delicately, from behind your chair, making you glance over at your spouse, while your dog laughs under his breath? Potpourri, anyone?

Resources

Regular Dog Food
Canidae
Solid Gold
Wysong
Pinnacle

Hypoallergenic Dog Food
Hill's Z/D and Ultra Z/D diets
CNM HA—from the prescription diet division of
Purina
EXclude—made by DVM dermatologics

Vegetarian Dog Food
Dick Van Patten's Natural Balance Vegetarian
Three Dog Bakery Vegetarian
www.threedogbakery.com
Wysong Vegan

Treats
Canidae Biscuits
Pork Skin Products
Old Mother Hubbard

Vegetarian Treats
Henry & Sons—www.henryandsons.com

Stress Relief
Rescue Remedy—www.rescueremedy.com/main

Toys
Kong
Kong Bounzer
Chuckit!
Humunga Tongue
Wiggly Giggly Ball

White Noise Products
The Sharper Image—www.sharperimage.com

Puppy Diapers
PetSmart—www.petsmart.com
PETCO—www.PETCO.com

Pet Photography & Fine Art
*Collie*ography—www.colleenpaige.com
Ron Burns—www.ronburns.com
Lisa Gizara—www.gizaraarts.com
J. Nicole Smith—www.thepetportraitstudio.com

Dog Safety
PupLight—www.puplight.com
Twist Step—www.twiststep.com

Dog Training & Behavior Modification
Colleen Paige—www.colleenpaige.com
Uncle Matty—www.unclematty.com

Pet Friendly Travel
Fido Friendly Travel Club—www.fidofriendlytravel-club.com
Midwest Airlines—www.midwestairlines.com

Dog-Friendly Publications
Fido Friendly Magazine—www.fidofriendly.com
Urban Dog Magazine—
www.urbandogmagazine.com
Animal Wellness Magazine—
www.animalwellnessmagazine.com
Dog Fancy—www.dogfancy.com

Dog Clothing & Accessories
G.W. Little—www.gwlittle.com
Wag Your Flag Shoppe—www.nationaldogday.com

Index

About the Author

ANIMAL BEHAVIORIST, COLUMNIST, AND TV and radio personality Colleen Paige has more than twenty years of dog behavior expertise. She started her career at the National Institute of Dog Training in Los Angeles, training celebrity and protection dogs under the expertise of her mentor, renowned dog trainer to the stars, Matthew "Uncle Matty" Margolis.

Colleen went on to be known as "The Animal Oracle" for her work with not only dogs but cats, elephants, wolves, bears, and tigers. Her approach to training combines the "Love & Praise" methods learned from her early education with a twist of her own soulful, unspoken understanding of animals. Over the years, she has earned numerous educational certifications and degrees in the medical, veterinary, and animal science fields.

Colleen is also the founder of National and International Dog Day on August 26, an annual day to celebrate the magic that all dogs bring to our lives and to thank them for their bravery and unconditional love. National Dog Day is a platform for the annual adoption of 10,000 shelter dogs in each participating country. In 2006, its first year, the program exceeded its goals in the U.S. by having more than 12,000 dogs adopted. She has also created National Puppy Day, National Cat Day, and National Wildlife Day.

In addition to her work with animals, Colleen enjoys singing, boating, songwriting, and poetry, and her artistic talents painting whimsical dogs, as well as her photography of pets, wildlife, and nature, have helped bring much-needed funding to the National Dog Day Foundation. Colleen currently lives in the beautiful Pacific Northwest with her husband and son and a menagerie of critters large and small. For more information, please visit www.colleenpaige.com and www.nationaldogday.com.